D0596263

THE
CRYSTALLINE
TRANSMISSION

A Synthesis of Light

Volume III

AURORA PRESS

P.O. Box 573   Santa Fe, N.M. 87504

First published in 1990 by:
Aurora Press
P.O. Box 573
Santa Fe, N.M. 87504

ISBN: 0--943358-33-7
Library of Congress Catalogue No: 89-081083

Cover Photo
© Gail Russell, 1990
Box 241
Taos, N.M. 87571

TABLE OF CONTENTS

SECTION II
THE PREDOMINANT POWER STONES

SECTION III
THE MASTER CRYSTALS

SECTION IV
MORE IMPORTANT HEALING STONES

SECTION V
FINAL NOTES UPON COMPLETION

ILLUSTRATIONS
AND PHOTOGRAPHS

PREFACE

The winds of change blow heavily in our times. We are all being faced with challenges that test our spiritual grit and can, if we are not clear within ourselves, threaten our very existence. All of the structures, as we have known them, are altering to meet the test of this time as this century closes. It seems as if nothing is stable anymore. Relationships, marriages, parenting, religion, politics, economics, business, and all other belief systems that are a part of our social programming are being tested against a higher frequency and a new standard of awareness and being. If the existing structure inherently possesses enough innate integrity of spirit, it will survive. If not, it is destined to change in order to be brought into alignment with the touchstone of truth indigenous to the Golden Age. If alteration is not possible, the outdated form will crumble along the wayside and become the debris from which the phoenix will rise.

Being alive now is indeed challenging and yet it provides us with opportunities for growth that only the immediate set

1

of circumstances can offer. The concepts that have been planetarily accepted for millenniums can no longer be allowed if our earth is to continue to survive. The ways in which we have related to ourselves and to one another need to be transformed in order to make way for the inner and outer peace that we are desperate for. As a race we are being forced to step forth into our power, not for the sake of power alone, but instead to dynamically express and share the peace and love that each one of us embodies at the very core of our beings. There are realities that need to be faced that can no longer be denied; the most obvious being that our planet is dying and will require a mass unified effort if we are to successfully cross the threshold into the Golden Age of Aquarius.

The Crystalline Transmission, which each one of us is a candidate for, is about fulfillment and completion. It is about identifying with that unchanging, undying, God Presence within our beings and integrating that Divine Essence into every facet of our physical reality. Then, and only then, will we be capable of honoring that same presence within all the other beings that exist, whether they are seen or unseen, incarnate or disincarnate, regardless of seemingly opposite race, sex, creed, color or difference. At this point, the vision and goal of *The Crystalline Transmission* is to acclimate and integrate our light bodies into our physical bodies. This vision will become the reality when our spiritual nature is consistently expressed into every minute facet of our lives. Then, that which we define as miracles will become the laws by which we learn to live.

This book, the completion of The Crystal Trilogy, leads us to a new beginning by offering us seeds of possibilities to be sown within our hearts. Throughout the conception, gestation and birth process of this information my own being has been transformed. More than with *Crystal Enlightenment*, Volume I or *Crystal Healing*, Volume II this book has offered me more joy and greater challenge. I have become increasingly aware that in order to relay this information, I needed to have the direct experience so that not only the message, but the essence of the transmission, could be relayed through the writing. If you have been wondering why it has taken me so long to complete this book, know that embracing the possibilities and experiencing the realities has been a personal process, requiring time as well as research and experimentation.

As I complete *The Crystalline Transmission, A Synthesis of Light*, Volume III, and offer it to you, I am now ever more aware of the role that crystals have played in our evolutionary process. They are incredible representations of that which we seek to be, unified spirit and matter. They are pure crystalline energies and color rays that affect our beings in ways that offer us greater hope, healing, beauty and light into our lives. The crystals and stones have been phenomenal teachers and healing agents in our process towards wholeness. They arrived on the scene in full force, at a time when we needed them the most. All of this, and yet, the time has come for us to acknowledge their place in our lives and open our arms to embrace the fact that what they symbolize and mean to us, exemplifies our own potential. It is no longer appropriate for us to empower any external object (or person) more than we empower the holy essence of our own inner source. Only by completely identifying with that internal source of power can we hope for the personal peace and security that will lay the foundation for planetary transformation.

In order to meet all of the incredible challenges that the next decade will present, it is necessary to be intimately connected to the greater cosmic whole. As we stabilize our identities in the God-Presence that feeds both polarities upon this earth, we will be capable of dealing with, adjusting to and recreating the world in which each one of us plays a vital part.

I offer to you on the following pages techniques and information that will assist in this process. As with each book that I write, I would like to say that all of the information is open to revision as I continue to learn and experience more. Also, with each book I write, I humbly place it in the hands of divine will to be received and utilized by those who are ready for it and who can in some way be served by it. I would also like to take this opportunity to thank all of you for being open to receive my soul essence through the Crystal Trilogy and for giving my life more purpose and meaning than I ever thought possible. Know that I love you and that I KNOW together we can perform great healing upon this planet.

SECTION I
THE CRYSTALLINE
TRANSMISSION

CHAPTER I
THE CRYSTALLINE TRANSMISSION

Human evolution is at a critical crossroads with the options clearly written on the wall. On the one hand, it is obvious that the earth's ecological system has been severely disrupted and our natural resources have been polluted and almost exhausted. As a race of beings we have not yet learned to live peacefully together as nations continually war upon one another with threats of nuclear extinction. These two factors alone point toward potential planetary holocaust. On the other hand however, the possibility also exists for spiritual light to be synthesized into every minute facet of our lives. This would indeed alter the very nature of life upon this planet and reward the earth with her crowning glory. As I see it, this is the only way to avoid the global destruction that conceivably awaits the human race. This book is dedicated to that hope and to the vision of human beings living in total attunement and harmony within themselves and with all other living creatures.

The term "The Crystalline Transmission" is synonymous with "blending spirit and matter" and "living heaven on earth. " This state of being is the eventual achievement of our human growth process and what each one of us has the opportunity to personally experience. Yes, history has recorded great individuals such as Akhnaton, Jesus Christ, Buddha, Mohammed, and Ghandi who lived in accordance with divine will and served as examples to us of this possibility. But now, the time demands that a much larger number of people receive their divine inheritance by aligning with their soul's essence and striving to live that truth in all of life's activities. Only then, will spiritual force be transmitted into the essence of the earth's substance to affect all living creatures and make possible planetary transformation.

The information that is presented in this section (as well as in The Predominant Power Stones section) has required years in this life as well as experience in many other lifetimes to gather. It is all about how we can activate and integrate our light bodies into our physical forms and blend the realities of both worlds, creating an entirely new way of being and order upon this earth. The ultimate end in working with crystals is to BECOME the crystalline reality, the light within the form, the spirit within matter. Yes, crystals and stones are used with great effectiveness to facilitate this process. In a sense they are not only the symbol of this reality but are as well the very tools and the teachers that help us to achieve it. But what is really important here must be clearly stated. Crystals are not the end unto themselves. Ultimately they are not to be empowered over the direct connection to our own soul source. The point is this: all we ever really need is to know who we are on the most primal essential level of our beings and aspire to manifest that divine presence in our lives.

The Crystalline Transmission

The time is upon us when the ancient mysteries can be made known to all of human-kind. The cosmic clock has struck the appointed hour and that which was once guarded as secret to only the high priests and priestesses, the fully ordained, and the entrusted few initiates can now be made available to all persons who could be bettered by it. A grand cycle of time is nearing its closure and with it comes tremendous possibilities and potential for each person incarnated on the planet today. Never before in the history of the human race has there been so much potential — for completion and fulfillment or for planetary destruction. The unveiling of the once concealed truth is a sacred journey that each individual now has the opportunity of undertaking. It involves conscious choice, determined direction, and committed action to clearly define and create a new reality out of the probable.

It is time for each being to take a sincere look into the inner sanctums of his/her own heart and discern that which is true, which has always been true and will continue to be true once this physical body crumbles into dust and the personality-ego structures fade into nothingness. Our solar system is completing a great galactic cycle and the earth and all of her offspring are intricately involved. With the closing of this grand revolution comes the most important opportunity that this world has ever seen. A phenomenal influx of spiritual force is radiating onto the earth and into our beings at every moment. It is necessary at this time to ready ourselves for those emanations and prepare the way so that the 'eternal truth' can find a homeland in our hearts and upon the earth. As we stabilize our identities in that 'undying essence of all things' the way will be made open for spiritual energies to manifest on a moment to moment basis in human consciousness and upon this physical plane.

The Crystalline Transmission is the process through which individuals ground and integrate their spiritual light bodies into their physical bodies. When this happens the divine presence becomes a conscious intregal part of every minute facet of daily life. As more and more individuals embody that light force they cannot help but transmit that frequency out into the world to assist and influence others in the same process. Crystals are powerful intermediaries for us to work with as we ready ourselves for complete spiritualization. They are the forms through which this reality is made manifest before our very eyes. In a crystal every atom, every molecule, each individual component vibrates in harmony with the divine force which has created it. They are true representations of the marriage of spirit and matter. If used correctly and with the right intention, crystals and healing stones can greatly assist us in accessing our own inner crystalline essence and in transmitting that spiritual light into every aspect of our human nature. The attunement and alignment that crystals innately possess can now also become ours if we are willing to reach inward and work for it. One of the most important keys in this process is our power and ability to 'consciously identify. '

THE POWER OF IDENTIFICATION

Nothing less will do in the times now upon us but to identify with the core essence of our beings, that which is eternally true and unconditionally loving. That is the tremendous opportunity at hand. How many times do we identify ourselves with less than that? How often are we totally caught up and identified with our pain, our emotions, our thoughts, our roles, our sex, our bodies and our limited sense of self? Thus far, the vast majority of our time and energy has been spent on experiencing the ways and means of the earth, of the emotions, of the mind and the individual sense of "I. " All of those things are destined to eventually pass away. We have become so immersed in the 'exclusively personal' that the majority of the time we function within the limitations of an ultimately false identity. Relating only to the individual sense of "I, " we are drastically influenced by the laws that govern the transient nature of the world. Instead, why not open ourselves up to live in accordance with the principles of spirit which govern those earthly laws?

We are now entering a new era in our growth process where it is possible to experience that the very God which we have prayed to in heaven exists within our own hearts. But how often do we go deep enough inside our hearts to find the place where we are truly ONE with the force of creation itself? How often do we relate to the impersonal nature of our beings, that which inspires the very pulse of life, not only on this planet but throughout the entire manifest and unmanifest realms of creation? How often do we still our minds enough to perceive and be nurtured by the Great Central Sun, which is the empowering generator for our solar sun? Are our hearts internally content and capable of embracing the vastness of our galaxy, of the universe of which the Milky Way is only a part, or of the boundless cosmos which fashions into being all of creation? It is possible to be not only connected with that source at all times but to be intimately identified with it, to draw forth its wisdom into our minds and its unconditional compassion into our hearts. Yes, the possibility is there, but to make it a reality very practical steps must be taken.

Only by constantly remembering our own divinity is it possible to assimilate the power by which we were created. Only by being identified with our source can we be strong enough to bring about conditions on earth in which love can flourish and peace prevail. Nothing but this holy connection can prepare us to keep our focus on what is being born, instead of being consumed with the fear of that which is destined to fall away. With our minds and hearts firmly focussed on the essence which is our very life, we will know that the changes that force us to 'let go' are but the labor pains birthing a new dawn; a new beginning on the horizon of our souls. As we let go of everything that no longer vibrates in harmony with spirit, channels will be reopened that have fallen into decay through misuse. Once these new avenues are reestablished the qualities of spirit will flow into our veins to nourish every cell with remembrance of purpose and clear identity in the divine.

The essential key to actualize the spiritual force upon the earth lies in conscious identification. Every time you say "I am . . . " realize that your identity is attached to whatever you say (or feel or think). For example, if I say "I am frustrated, " I have identified my being with frustration and I become that emotional state. I have defined my identity to a very limited uncomfortable condition and there I stay until something (which is usually out of my personal realm of control) happens or I choose to redefine myself.

As a race we have so many subconscious predefined identities that it requires a diligent effort to detach ourselves from these notions and consciously reidentify. And when we do, we can choose what we become identified with and what we attach our beings to. Yes, we can become great in our society and in this world if we really choose that, we can become successful and financially secure if that is the chosen direction, we can literally redefine and recreate ourselves in whatever manner we decide. But, what is the pure essence within each one of us that calls out for acknowledgment, that 'absolute' which is the only presence that can bring forth peace, love, and truth into our beings? Once we have identified with that God presence within, everything else involved with our mental, emotional, and physical realities can readjust and come into alignment with a new sense of order. It is time to reevaluate, redetermine and refocus our life force on this chosen priority. That is the hope that will give birth to an entirely new all encompassing sense of self and allow the earth to conceive a prodigy worthy of her long term efforts.

The Crystalline Transmission

There are many subconscious programs that we have unwillingly and unknowingly become attached to that must be looked at and dealt with honestly and directly. One of the most powerful is the pattern of attack-defend-protect. This program is the seed of every war the earth has ever known and has been genetically carried on in the human race for thousands of years. This pattern is so strong that it is acted out automatically and is now taking on global proportions only because it is continuously being dramatized in our personal lives and individual relationships. It is because we are identified with less than our true selves that we take things so personally and feel as if we are being individually attacked. Even if another person actually verbally offends or attacks us, we have the choice whether to accept it or not. If our identities are not attuned to the essence which we truly are, chances will be that we involuntarily react to the program of attack. Out of trying to defend our fragile egos, we protect ourselves by either retreating with fear into insecurity, or by attacking back with anger and violence.

The pathway of the Crystalline Transmission is one of self-mastery. We must consciously choose to reidentify and empower our love over all else — especially over our subconscious identification with fear and anger. It is so easy to try and prove ourselves right instead of attempting to create peace, to make our point to unlistening ears instead of reaching into ourselves for greater understanding, or to come out on top of the battle or conflict instead of striving for harmony. It is necessary for us to now change the age old genetic programs that operate under the laws and bylaws of fear. In doing so, the very foundation of life as we have known it will need to be reorganized and recreated in a way that harmonizes with the impersonal life-giving essence of all things. This new way of existence is not based upon the the limited definitions of reality as we have been taught. It is based instead upon the laws of spirit working in harmony with humanity.

The genetic program of attack-defend-protect must be broken within us. If we are not at peace within ourselves, how can we attempt to create peace even in the relationships that are closest to us — be it parent-child, husband-wife, friend, neighbor or countryman? If we are to survive as a race, it is mandatory at this point in time that this pattern be altered and consciously reprogrammed with a deep inner sense of security in the divine. It is of the utmost importance to consolidate our energies, individually and together, and focus on that aspect of our beings that is connected to infinite spirit. It is time to consciously identify with that sacred inner source and continuously, moment to moment, draw our only true security and healing energy from the sole place that it actually exists, within the crystalline essence of our own beings.

When a person clearly and consciously identifies with the "essence of all that is" within his/her own inner self, and strives to live that truth, new seeds are planted that are destined to blossom forth into fruits that will fulfill and nurture all aspects of the human self. When you affirm and believe "I am that essence, I am" great transformation occurs, not only within the inner sanctums of your own personal being but outward, into all of your relationships and worldly affairs.

SURRENDERING TO THE DIVINE IMPERSONAL

To relate to and identify with the impersonality of our divine nature does not in any way mean that we will lose conection with the natural concerns of daily life. It does not mean that all of the personal matters that are important to us will not be attended to. We will not become indifferent to this physical world, which is the spirit's most challenging training ground, and of which we are obviously pupils. What it can mean however is that we choose to permeate our physical reality with that supreme essence so that we may become aligned with the wondrous and miraculous. It is important for us now, as evolving human-light beings, to break out of the sphere of being solely personal on a limited human level, and infiltrate the divine impersonal into our beings to assist us in governing all of our human interests. This essential substance is the very force which enables our hearts to beat, our bodies to carry on incredible functions, while giving our minds the impetus to create conscious thoughts. On a larger scale, this energy simultaneously causes the earth to spin on its axis and rotate around the sun, while orchestrating the entire galaxy's perfected motion. If this underlying presence pervades and gives movement and life to all that is, can we not trust it to preside over and reorder our seemingly important worldly affairs?

That God-force is present within all things and as human-light beings we are capable of acknowledging it as our true identity — that which we were before this life (or any human life), and that which we will continue to be when this earth and our sun no longer exist. But how is it possible to bring the ultimate divinity into the humanly personal? By what means do we usher spirit into our beings, into our very nerves, into each and every cell? Surely it is only through this type of divine intervention that generations of genetic coding based in lack, insecurity, pain, and war can be transmuted and reprogrammed.

Using crystals as our examples and teachers we can see that it is possible for the form to manifest the light, for each molecule to align in perfect order, for every atom to vibrate at a common frequency. Yes, it is possible for us, too, to align the very fiber in our bodies, every thought within our minds and each feeling emanating from our hearts to this common source. What is required to do so is sincere effort, determination and most importantly — openness.

It is impractical for us to try to use our minds and think of what the divine presence in human affairs would be like. Our minds have not yet been programmed in that way. It is difficult for us to perceive what the outcome of this mergence will look like, feel like, or become when it has not yet been embraced within the realm of personal experience. At this point even our wildest imagination falls short of conceptualizing that reality. The best we can do at this stage is create an opening in our minds, hearts and bodies for this presence to be actualized. This state of openness creates a clear, free space within our beings that welcomes in the influx of pure essential force. It is a conscious invitation with an assured R.S.V.P. This open space is totally free from previous identification and potent with potential and possibilities.

It is in a holy state of internal silence and peace that this presence simply "becomes" a part of you. Meditative quiet time is required for this invitation to be responded to. Personal discipline is required to still the mind and open the heart to its conception. But the guarantee is there. As the foundation for this new identity is formed, life will change and come into accordance with the prevailing peace of this holy presence. Do not try to define the ways and means that it will manifest — just be open and allow 'it' to be superimposed over all of the old patterns and pain. The rest will follow naturally and bear the fruits of divinity. This is the first phase in the process of the Crystalline Transmission. It is like the engagement period before the marriage of the light body and the physical body.

PRACTICALITIES AND PREREQUISITES

The art, science and technology of grounding the light body into the physical body has several prerequisites and practical steps involved. First, as discussed above, a conscious opening is made as we humbly bow and surrender at the altar of the Impersonal Divine. It is then usually necessary to undergo a certain amount of cleansing, clearing and letting go of programmed beliefs about the nature of life and the world of which we are a part. The mind needs to be consciously worked with and reprogrammed. Focussed meditation in which affirmation, confirmation, and identification with the sacred "I am" essence lays the foundation upon which the light body can enter the into mental realm.

Our fragile human hearts also need healing and rejuvenation. For this reason, *Crystal Healing*, Volume II was written with the ways and means made available to emotionally restore and redefine ourselves. As our hearts come to understand the purpose for which we have undergone human pain, new faith and hope will renew our power to love, ever more deeply and completely than we can now imagine.

The physical body must also be diligently worked with to prepare it for the massive influx of spiritual energy as the light body descends into matter. A daily workout to strengthen the muscles and organs, deep breathing exercises to increase oxygenation, increased pure water intake, proper nutrition, and joyful play time are all required on the physical level.

It is important to realize here that the initial phases of cleansing, letting go, healing, and strengthening are very important in this over all process. Ample time and energy should be given to these preparatory stages before rushing into the actual exercises and initiation layouts (soon to be given in this book) to literally usher the light body into the physical body. Personal preparation may require weeks, months, or even years before practicing the forthcoming Sun Meditations, working with the Predominate Power Stone Layout or activating the non-physical chakras. **If not adequately prepared, much more harm than good can occur.** Take it slow and receive clear guidance before embarking into experience with these upcoming advanced procedures. Once the initial prerequisites are met, candidacy for the Crystalline Transmission is upon you!

Several remarkable changes will become obvious as these preparatory stages are completed and the light body begins its descent. First, a certain degree of detachment to the illusionary workings and ways of the world naturally develops. It is not that you won't care, it is rather that you will begin to see life with a greater perspective and will have more faith that everything will work out perfectly. Increased lightness and joy, a genuine but detached concern, a greater sense of humor, and an obvious growing compassion are all symptoms of the Crystalline Transmission. You will gain an inner security that negates whatever fear might arise and an ability to acknowledge and appreciate the beauty of life in all of its varied expressions. Most importantly, an innate undying trust in the cosmic power which created your very being will become your strength and show you your purpose. Watch for these changes in yourself. The first sign will be greater inner peace and a true sense of gratitude for this experience called human life.

CHAPTER II

THE TWELVE CHAKRA SYSTEM

Throughout the last few thousand years most members of our human race have been primarily engrossed in experiencing those things in and of the physical world. During this time we have been utilizing eight main chakra centers. But now, as our galaxy completes its grand revolution around the Great Central Sun, a new Golden Age commences. The opportunity is at hand where, as human light beings, it is possible to assimilate the abundance of cosmic rays that the Great Central Sun now blesses our planet with. If utilized properly, these solar emanations can pierce the veiling darkness in our minds so that fear no longer consumes our consciousness. In order to do this, and become one with the essence of all things, it is necessary to activate three transpersonal chakra centers that exist above the crown chakra. If this energy is then to become a living, breathing part of our existence upon this material plane, the Earth Star Chakra approximately six inches below the soles of the feet, must also be activated.

Thus, we have four more energy centers to acknowledge, work with and reawaken.

ADVANCED SKULL STRUCTURES

In my years of direct experience and study of the Egyptian and Peruvian remnants of the ancient civilizations of Atlantis and Lemuria, it has become evident that the advanced beings who first inhabited this planet embodied a very different physical structure than what we now observe in humankind. (For further reference read The Earthkeepers, *Crystal Healing*, Volume II pages. 156-161). When these evolved Elders of our race entered into human incarnation they brought with them the ability to maintain a constant attunement to the energy forces of light radiating from the luminous core of Mother Milky Way. In those times the spiritual laws manifested upon the earthplane and those beings lived in harmony with both the earth and the heavens. Their heads were developed in such a way that two other energy centers were encompassed within their brain structures, thus incorporating into physicality the embodiment of higher consciousness. Today representations of these advanced skulls can be seen in the Cairo Museum as well as in Peruvian and Mayan relics. In recent times benevolent extraterrestrial beings have also been portrayed with elongated heads by the brilliant creative minds who brought to us *E.T.* and *Close Encounters of the Third Kind*. Being exposed through the mass media to advanced beings with mature brain structures such as these is yet another way that the divine intelligence has of rekindling our awakening and lifting the veils in our consciousness.

A common question is asked concerning the destiny of our ancient ancestors which I will address to the best of my ability. As time went on the Elder race eventually interbred

ADVANCED SKULL STRUCTURES
AND
THE TRANSPERSONAL CHAKRAS

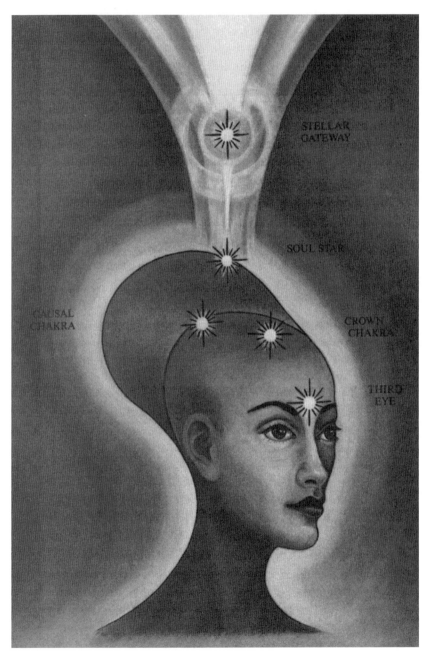

with the primates evolving upon the earth. This genetic mixing diluted their ability to stay attuned with the Divine Essence and the head structures changed, as did the consciousness that they embodied.

These beings originally incarnated at the beginning of this great time cycle when the cosmic emanations radiating from the Great Central Sun were at a peak. Throughout the thousands of years in between, the learning process has been one that involved the densifying of spiritual force into slow moving time and space. Being consumed in physicality the memory veils thickened and ages of forgetfulness followed. Now, as that cycle completes itself, the earth once again receives an abundance of cosmic rays from the center of our galaxy. It is not likely that our head structures will actually change, even though at this point anything can happen. More importantly, the possibility now exists to reactivate these higher chakra centers and reawaken the states of consciousness that they can emit.

In the ancient days all twelve of the chakras were in an active state and the entire rainbow ray of consciousness was in full manifested expression. It was then that the advanced Elders were at-one with the very forces of creation and used the universal energies available to them to propagate incredible life forms upon this planet. As the natural destined cycle of devolution occurred, consciousness became focussed on the personal sense of self, and the three upper chakras fell into a state of dormancy. No longer was the divine essence identified with as the 'Self.' Instead, the infinite presence was forgotten and the individual persons related to a God or Gods that were separate from themselves. It was as if the reality of spirit merely became a vague reflection, something that could be related to only outside of personal experience or expression.

This pattern of ego (or individual identification) created the cycles of rebirth, of pain, and of lonely separation that have become the reality for those living upon this earth plane. When humans only have a dull mirrored reflection of the truth, instead of complete personal acknowledgment and access to it, fear is the natural outcome. If life's energy is claimed solely for individual purpose and prestige, the Divine Essence becomes so clouded that only shadows of grey are mirrored in one's life. An individual that relates exclusively to his/her own limited sense of power, instead of with the omnipotent dominion of the divine, is destined to face the ultimate fear of personal death and extinction. The reality is, everything else but that divine impersonal presence will eventually crumble at the hands of time and space and pass away.

And yet, this cycle that involved veiled forgetfulness is the very process through which new breeds of beings evolve and truly come to know the right use of power and the glory of their Oneness. It is not for us to condemn or feel guilty about our experiences upon the earthplane, whatever they might have been. It is more that we can now reap the harvest of this cycle and rekindle the forces that will realign our souls and activate our light bodies. Now is the time to rejoice, a time of potential fulfillment and completion, a time of realignment and attunement to that which has guided us safely through the darkened hours of the night.

In the days which are upon us the radiations of the great galactic sun once again showers all living things upon the earth with increased cosmic energy. With this heavenly help we have the potential to once again synthesize the light forces of the upper chakras and integrate into states of expanded consciousness all of the lessons that the earth plane cycle has taught us. Yes, the awareness will be different now than it was thousands of years ago when these chakras were last functioning. We have much to contribute, much to add to the knowledge of how to live spirit in human form. Our soul's descent into matter was for a very special purpose which can now be realized and accomplished if enough individuals have courage, readapt to the heavenly influences, and welcome the changes that will result in our ultimate unfoldment.

THE THREE TRANSPERSONAL CHAKRAS

The three upper transpersonal energy centers are herein named The Soul Star, The Causal Chakra and the Stellar Gateway (see illustration, page 21). Each one of these chakras has a specific purpose in enabling the Divine Impersonal Essence to be actualized and assimilated into the eight chakras currently existing in the human form. Before elaborating on the upper chakras, first let us briefly review those energy centers that are most familiar to us. The system that is used in crystal healing is slightly different than the more commonly known system originating in India in that eight instead of seven chakras are utilized. In the Vedic system the navel and the solar plexus are combined together as only one chakra, whereas in crystal healing each one of these centers constitute their own energy and individual purpose. These eight chakras will be described as if they were opened, balanced, in harmonious alignment with all of the other chakras, and functioning at their optimum.

The crown chakra is located at the center top of the head and is the highest seat of consciousness encased within the physical brain structure. It serves a double function. First, it is the gateway through which individual human consciousness can 'beam out' to connect with the three transpersonal chakras. Secondly, the crown chakra is the place where the impersonal divine energy can become defined into individuality and personal purpose. It is through the crown that the state of 'oneness' can be assimilated and channeled into the rest of the physical chakras. This chakra has the potential of functioning as a double-helix vortex; with energy

The Twelve Chakra System

spiraling out to connect with greater wholeness while simultaneously directing that energy into physicality.

The third eye center exists between the eyebrows and is called 'the eye of the soul.' It is where the divine perfection can be witnessed within all earthly matters. This chakra anchors the mind to inner knowing, intuition and wisdom. There is an etheric bridge that can be consciously built to connect the third eye to the crown chakra. Once constructed, the individual's personal divine purpose and connection to the infinite is constantly witnessed by the third eye while in the midst of physical activity.

The throat chakra is located in the nook where the clavicle bones meet. This energy center exists between the head and the heart and is to be used for clear verbal expression of what is thought and felt. The power of the word, of sound, and of verbal manifestation is actualized through this chakra.

The heart chakra is found in the center of the chest and is associated with the power of unconditional love. It is here that the Divine Impersonal finds its greatest human expression in compassion.

The solar plexus is located where the sternum ends, the ribs separate and the abdominal cavity begins. Ideally, the solar plexus functions in harmony with its higher octave, the heart. In so doing, love is felt towards all things related to the earth.

The navel chakra, at the belly button, is the energy center through which the Divine Essence can find human expression through physical manifestation. It is here where one's personal sense of power can assimilate cosmic frequencies and materialize those energies into physical creations and the attainment of goals.

The sexual or second chakra is located half way between the pubic bone and the navel point. Life producing creative energy is generated here which can be utilized in the actual creation of physical life or in other focussed and channeled outlets. Great rejuvenation, regeneration and revitalization of the physical body can be stimulated through this energy center.

The base chakra is found between the anus and the sex organs with associated points in the middle of the pubic bone and at the center of each groin. This chakra is the grounding point through which the Divine Essence takes up permanent residence in the human body, superimposing the consciousness of the crown and the unconditional love of the heart over the fight/flight instincts of animalistic survival.

There are also secondary chakras in the palm of each hand, at the shoulders, elbows, knees, and on the soles of the feet — all of which can be consciously used to focus spiritual energy. But before any of the above energy centers can be used to their maximum capacity the three transpersonal chakras and the Earth Star must be activated. Then, fully conscious beings emerge, manifesting all-around perfection inclusive of the Divine Impersonal and the intimately personal.

Before continuing with information on the three transpersonal chakras I would like to emphasize that even though I have done years of extensive research on these energy centers, I do not yet feel that the knowledge is complete. I am grateful to share what I have learned thus far and must also add that the full awareness of these upper chakras comes only through personal experience, which we are all in the process of undergoing. As each one of us consciously activates these chakras complete knowledge of them will come into existence and be transmitted into our lives on a moment to moment basis. Also, because each individual's head structure varies in size, shape, and proportion, the exact location of these chakra points will slightly differ as well. With that clarification stated I will now gladly share with you what I have learned through experiential research with the three transpersonal energy centers.

THE STELLAR GATEWAY

The Stellar Gateway is located approximately twelve inches above the top of the head and to my knowledge at this time is the highest chakra that can be incorporated into the human system. This chakra is activated with two essential elements. One is the vitalizing cosmic rays emanating from the Great Central Sun, which our planet and our beings are now receiving. The second critical element required to reignite the Stellar Gateway is the power of the human will focussed in conscious intention. With both of these components present, a human-light being is capable of spiritually nurturing all aspects of the self by maintaining a direct link to the Divine Impersonal.

With this chakra in a dormant state as it has been, it is almost impossible to completely identify one's being with that which is defined as "God. " But, as the Stellar Gateway opens unified oneness can be personally experienced. This is the ultimate of all religious experiences, in which one intimately identifies with the undeniably real, yet intangible, shapeless, unnameable presence within all things. This is not merely a state of perception. It is rather an experience of at-one-ment which qualifies one to boldly, yet without ego, affirm "I am THAT, I am. "

Communication is the key to unlock the secrets of the cosmic stellar spaces that can activate this chakra. Communication is a two way transference of energy where each party transmits and receives. This spiritual exchange, wherein the individual soul communes with the infinite spirit, is the means through which the Stellar Chakra can be integrated into the human system. The soul must acknowledge and be open to receive the experience of oneness. The mind and heart must be capable of detaching from inferior identities associated with the personality and ego structures. Personal quiet time must be taken to prioritize this as it becomes a physical reality. When the reception channels are clear and open, the universe will respond by lifting the awareness up out of the realms of the limited personal and into stellar spaces where the creative force exists in harmonious union with all things.

Once this experience is attained the stellar presence can be relayed back into all of the lower chakra centers (if they maintain harmonious alignment and balance). With daily meditation, the Stellar Chakra will transmit cosmic rays into the consciousness, quicken the nerve fibers, and literally elevate the atomical frequencies of the physical body. With determined effort, the Stellar Gateway will remain open and that state of oneness with the entire cosmic creation can be grounded into earthly functionings. The result is living wisdom, undying compassion and a constant permanent connection to divine guidance in human affairs.

Even in the advanced skull structures of the ancient ones, the Stellar Chakra was not encompassed in the brain and existed outside of the body. It has always been the chakra which was incapable of becoming attached to any one individual identification. The Stellar Gateway maintains supreme impersonality, that which holds the cosmos in impeccable order and perfection. The state of consciousness that it conveys can never belong to only one thing for it is the very force which is all things. Through activation of this chakra that ultimate consciousness can be experienced by human-light beings. But, to then integrate that cosmic frequency into the realm of the human soul, the Soul Star must then be activated and aligned with the Stellar Chakra.

THE SOUL STAR

The Soul Star is located approximately six inches above the top of the head and is the interconnecting link between the Stellar Gateway and the eight human chakras. It is the bridge between the impersonal essence and the personal reality, the spiritual and the physical, the heavens and the earth. The Soul Star exists between the Stellar Gateway and the Causal and Crown Chakras (see illustration, page 21).

It is now above the top of the head but in ancient times this chakra center was located within the mature brain structures which housed the consciousness of cosmic oneness. Today the Soul Star is being slightly activated merely by being exposed to the increased emanations radiating from the great central sun. It is further stimulated and awakened by using the powerful crystalline entity of Selenite (more information on Selenite is given in The Predominant Power Stone Section on page 59).

The highest and most powerful energy we are aware of in the third dimension is light. The refined frequency of light is the medium through which impersonal cosmic emanations can enter into the physical plane. The Soul Star is the chakra that translates the infinite energy accessible at the Stellar Gateway and filters it into the soul level of the human-light being. It's unique ability and purpose is to gather the detached essence of the cosmos and personalize it into the domain of the human soul. As boundless cosmic energy is densified, the Soul Star goes to work and weaves a spiritual body out of light. Thus, the means is created through which an individual can unify the vastness of the omnipotent ONE creative power with the humanly personal.

The number eleven is one of the master numbers and symbolizes a new beginning on a higher octave. Restored alignment with this powerful eleventh energy center indicates that a new fabric of life can be woven as the threads of cosmic force are delicately intertwined with the soul essence of humanness. Unless this chakra is activated, it is unlikely that the internal realization of Oneness would ever manifest into worldly activity. Once resurrected, the Soul Star is capable of maintaining an open channel through which spiritual inspiration can flow into personal expression. The whole concept of The Crystalline Transmission is very much related to the number eleven. At this point it represents the potential that we all have to live life in an entirely new way, on a higher level. By creating a light body out of stellar frequencies and then gently guiding that force into the human chakra system, we will octavate (activate on a higher octave) physical reality. When cosmic energy is transmitted by conscious life forms (such as we are) great healing will occur and the hearts of others will be lightened by this divine presence emanating from our beings.

Having the unique ability to assimilate light, the Soul Star is highly susceptible to solar rays. For this reason the Sun Meditations (detailed on page 46) can be practiced to further activate this vital energy center. As the solar-stellar rays are assimilated one will begin to feel the personal connection to the infinite source of energy responsible for creating all life. But, if that divine impersonal love and wisdom is to be integrated into the multi-dimensional ways and means of life on earth, it is mandatory that the Earth Star Chakra, located below the soles of the feet also be activated. (Specific information on the Earth Star is forthcoming). The Soul Star and the Earth Star are complementary halves of the same whole, each allowing the other full glorified expression. If the Soul Star is activated and the Earth Star is not, the light will never find its perfected completion in the spiritualization of matter.

The Soul Star can be an escape route for those who may have an internal sense of oneness but thus far have not had the courage or the capabilities to manifest that unity in their lives. It is possible to beam one's consciousness into the lower levels of the Soul Star and relate only to the light. But, in so doing, imbalance and disorientation is the outcome and it eventually becomes even more difficult to accept the challenge of fully functioning in the world. Even so, it is not possible to completely merge solely with the stellar realms as long as there are lessons to learn on the physical plane. The illusions of the earth then become like a magnet that is held in play by resistance to it. Soul Star escape routes eventually create greater bondage to the earth.

It is understandable why evolved sensitive souls would prefer to hang out in the light instead of choosing to fully enter into the conditions of pain upon the earth. Perhaps for a time it was necessary to be exclusively identified with the light. But the time is upon us when we now can relate to the earth in a brand new way; we can embrace the entire whole. The soul's essence is intimately connected to the omnipresent oneness that has become personalized at the Soul Star. When this chakra is activated our sense of connection with all things will result in a new relationship with the earth. When we are capable of knowing that all things share the same spiritual essence, unconditional love is felt for everything; the good as well as " bad, " the light and the dark, the sadness and the pain, and all creatures great or small. This unification of the complementary aspects of yin and yang within ourselves will reflect out into the world and close the widened gaps of separateness between us. In this way the light is woven into the earth and full scale transformation can occur.

An important factor in activating the Soul Star is psychic cleansing. There is a need to clean out the mental pollution in the Soul Star area before the stellar-solar rays can be transmitted. Lower astral travels that occur in dream states, depressed states of mind, over indulgence of hallucinogenic drugs, and unhealthy thoughts that can include self-oriented fantasy, projection or imagination can leave a shadowed cloud in the area above the top of the head. These levels of the lower astral mind can be cleared by visualizing a golden white orb of energy radiating above the crown chakra. As the concentration is held over the top of the head to dissolve astral pollution, it is also important to ground the energies by placing Black Tourmaline at the soles of the feet. When the Soul Star space is cleared of infringing thoughtforms, the Divine Essence can more easily enter into the auric field bringing with it spiritual frequencies and high ethical standards.

It is into the light of the Soul Star that the soul enters when the physical body dies and where it gains perspective on its evolutionary process. The ultimate initiation is to maintain a conscious connection to the source while going through the death experience; in other words to have a firm identification with that essence within that never dies. It is only because over-identification is made with the physical plane that this connection is fractured and the terrifying fear of death exists. These fears are deeply ingrained on a genetic level and have been passed down through generations. They begin to shift as energy from the Soul Star is consciously transmitted into these programmed codes in the cells. The Sun Meditations (page 46) provide an excellent exercise through which this type of cellular transformation can be achieved.

When the Soul Star is fully activated it becomes a double-helix vortex with energy from the Stellar realms coming into physical reality while personal identification is being projected out to maintain constant connection with the grand source of all things. (As previously stated, the crown chakra also has this ability). The total process involved in The Crystalline Transmission is not just the raising of the kundalini and elevating the animal instincts of the physical body into the higher consciousness centers. It is also inclusive of the descent of omnipresent spiritual force through the Stellar Chakra and into the individuation at the Soul Star. Once energy is established there it can then be relayed into the crown and infiltrate into the entire rainbow ray chakra system, with the final destination at the Earth Star grounding spiritual force into the roots of humanity.

The next step in the descent of spirit into perfected form is performed by the action of The Causal Chakra. How is it possible to harness the powers of the mind to contribute in the Crystalline Transmission? How can that pure source energy create the mental blueprint for materialization? Read on as the third transpersonal chakra is revealed and these questions answered.

THE CAUSAL CHAKRA

In ancient days this chakra was encased within the advanced brain structure. Today it is located at the center back of the head, approximately three to four inches behind the crown chakra (see illustration, page 21). This location is also the site of a main acupuncture point that can be stimulated in life-death situations and/or when an even flow of energy needs to be created within the brain. As the Causal Chakra is reawakened more relevant and pertinent uses will be discovered for this acupressure point.

The power of the mind to create conscious thought forms is paralleled only with the mighty strength of love generated at the heart chakra. If the mind is disciplined and trained to be receptive to subtle frequencies it can be the greatest tool through which spiritual energies can manifest into brilliant ideas. On the other hand, if the mind is not properly instructed and remains uncontrolled it will run rampant and can be the greatest detriment in the development of higher consciousness. The Causal Chakra is the third of the transpersonal chakras and is the energy center through which the Impersonal Divine can manifest in subtle thought patterns. This energy center literally has the capacity to usher the soul force into the mental body to be further utilized in corporal functions. But, before this chakra can be activated and aligned with the Stellar Gateway and the Soul Star a certain degree of dominion over the mind must be developed. Weeks, months or years of meditative practice and self-mastery over the lower workings of the mind would precede full activation of the Causal Chakra. If the soul force is to fully enter into the mental plane, disassociation from programmed belief systems and linear based concepts, as well as conscious reprogramming are required prerequisites.

The mind must be open and responsive, stilled and quieted before the Soul Star can transmit cosmic frequencies into this energy center to conceive purified thought. Peace of mind and mental silence are the keys to activate the Causal Chakra and seed the stellar transmissions into our thinking modes.

As spiritual energy further densifies, the light transmitted from the Soul Star stimulates this important chakra and gives birth to original thought imbued with spiritual inspiration. This causal nucleus is associated with the highest most subtle level of the mind where thoughts spring forth from spirit, unencumbered with previous association. It is from within the Causal Chakra that thoughts can be constructed that maintain true integrity with the force that created them. When spiritual elements converge to create mental substance the outcome is an inner knowing of the laws that govern the miraculous.

Our thoughts become the blueprints for what will manifest on the physical plane and in our lives. The incredible activity of the mind consumes a vast amount of energy. Many thoughts have very little value and never even register in the realm of the akasha or the soul. Once the Causal Chakra is activated and aligned with the Soul Star the meaningless wanderings and egotistical ramblings of the mind give way to the pure creations originating from the source. This quality of thought alters perception and broadens the horizon of consciousness in a way that invites spiritual meaning into all inferior mental patterns and programs. As this chakra is activated the light of the soul is superimposed and infiltrated into and through every minute nick and cranny of the conscious and subconscious minds. The result is miraculous and transformative as those impressions take on physical dimension.

The Stellar Gate is the apex of these upper chakras, expanding and extending the human awareness into the realm of the divine. It beams out into the omniscient vastness of infinity. The Soul Star transmits in both directions; spiraling upward to contact cosmic energies while simultaneously bridging the light of the soul into the mind. The Causal Chakra is an inward vortex and is the base point for the two upper chakras. It is like the landing pad for spiritual energies to ground and formulate conscious perception.

The nature of the Causal Chakra is silent peace. It is like the quietude that surrounds a seed within the earth in the winter months. It is a perpetual open womb space through which unlimited potential sleeps, awaiting to be germinated with cosmic impressions. It is there, in the core of that serenity, that the stellar impressions relayed through the Soul Star find fertile ground, connecting and aligning the impersonal with the finest level of human thought. The rest of the eight chakras further distribute that energy resulting in full rainbow ray expression into the crux and core of human matter.

Meditation at the Causal Chakra point facilitates attunement to the inner realm of the soul and sweet silent peace of mind is achieved. Continued focus upon this energy center during meditation with Kyanite will gradually construct a sanctuary in the mind. This is where the Divine Essence can be reflected upon, renewing and restoring personal identification with spirit and soothing the turbulent tides of life. It will take time before those seeds of universal consciousness planted in the potent ground of the Causal Chakra sprout into ideas or concepts. Time is always needed for germination and gestation to take place. In the meantime the peace and calmness can be assimilated into very deep levels of the human psyche. (For more specific information on how to activate this vital chakra center read Kyanite in the Predominate Power Stone Section on pages 71-79).

Once activated the Causal Chakra becomes like an oasis of blue that stays clear and calm no matter what else is going on. Within the incredible activity of the mind involved with the trials and tribulations of the world, the Causal Chakra is a source of constant calm and comfort. As it develops, the Causal Chakra has the capacity to keep one connected to the soul's presence while in the midst of the noise and confusion of life. Once the Causal Chakra is activated and its frequency stabilized, the mind will maintain a secure commitment to the divine presence and proper integration of the light at the Soul Star will be ensured. With absolute awareness of the universal source while in the midst of whatever activity the mind might engage itself with, spiritual meaning is achieved in this ever changing passage of time in the dimension of space.

But how is it possible for that stellar energy seeded within the causal levels of the mind to become an intregal part of the natural forces existing on the earthplane? How can cosmic energy be grounded in such a way that absolute integrity is maintained in its material manifestation? The way, the means and the key lies in the simultaneous activation of the Earth Star.

THE TWELVE CHAKRA SYSTEM

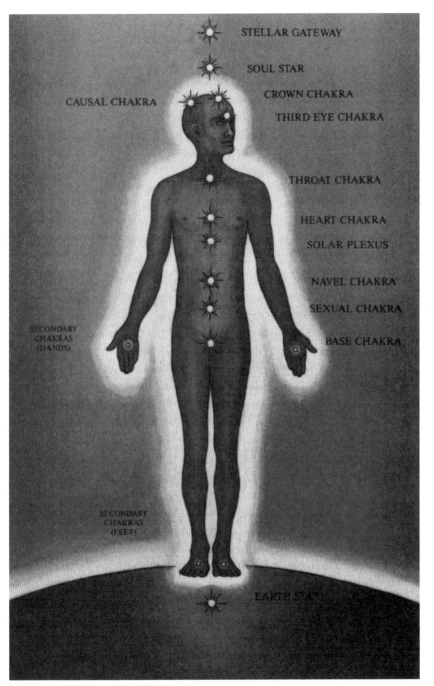

STELLAR GATEWAY

SOUL STAR

CAUSAL CHAKRA

CROWN CHAKRA

THIRD EYE CHAKRA

THROAT CHAKRA

HEART CHAKRA

SOLAR PLEXUS

NAVEL CHAKRA

SEXUAL CHAKRA

SECONDARY
CHAKRAS
(HANDS)

BASE CHAKRA

SECONDARY
CHAKRAS
(FEET)

EARTH STAR

THE EARTH STAR

Located approximately six inches below the soles of the feet is the Earth Star. Between the Causal Chakra and the Earth Star exist the eight chakras which we have previously reviewed. Corresponding to the Earth Star point are energy centers found at the soles of the feet. The two sole chakras and the Earth Star form a triangle pointing downward that channels the Divine Essence not only through the physical body but into the very roots of a human-light being's relationship to the Earth. The re-creation of matter is dependent upon those stellar rays infiltrating into the very substance comprising the earth.

In activating the Earth Star, the very nature of physicality becomes aligned and attuned to the life producing force of creation itself. When individuals can walk upon this earth and vibrate at that frequency the Crystalline Transmission will become a reality, the living proof of perfected self-mastery. The Earth Star, when fully activated and aligned with the three upper transpersonal chakras, weaves the golden white threads of the Impersonal Divine into and through the realm of the humanly personal, creating a new fabric of worldly existence. This is the role that we all can play in the contribution to the spiritualization of our earth.

The physical plane is governed by the laws of polarity. The Earth Star is the vital polarity point through which the divine consciousness of the Stellar Gateway, the Soul Star and the Causal Chakra attains full expression. In the conscious activation of the upper three chakras it is necessary to simultaneously activate the Earth Star. Indeed, it is only possible to stimulate the Earth Star with the cosmic rays emanating from the transpersonal chakras. Likewise, the consciousness associated with the higher energy centers yearns to find ultimate fulfillment in the harvesting of the soular seeds rooted in the elements of matter. The balance and harmony created between the transpersonal chakras above the top of the head, and the Earth Star below the soles of the feet, establishes the proper polarity through which the holy presence of the eternal force can elevate and renew the earth. Allow me to use the example of the pyramids to further explain. The pyramids in Egypt are structures that were built by the ancient ones (whom we have previously made mention of) who encompassed the consciousness of the transpersonal within their brain-skull structures. The pyramids are perfect geometric forms through which cosmic emanations were literally channeled into earth's material substance. The axis of the earth has slightly tilted since the pyramids were built and they are no longer in direct alignment to the emanations of the star systems that they were originally fine-tuned with. Even so, they stand unto this day as a manifestation of the potential of physical forms transmitting cosmic energies into the earth.

What is most interesting in the experiential study of the pyramids in Egypt is that they all had chambers either at the ground level or beneath the earth. It is as if their makers knew that in order to channel cosmic frequencies into the earth they needed to create compartments on or beneath the ground level to receive and substantiate stellar transmissions. It is a common misconception that the pyramids were used as burial tombs. Instead, the inner chambers were used as initiation sanctuaries where the soul force of the initiates would either consciously transcend the physical plane, or in the case of the lower chambers, ground their essence into the roots of the earth.

The Step Pyramid and the Pyramid of Unas at Saqqara both exhibit underground chambers. The Red Pyramid at Dahshur has two interior chambers on the ground level. Two internal chambers beneath the surface of the earth and one on the ground level have been found in the Bent Pyramid of

Snefru. The collapsed Pyramid of Meidum has only one chamber on the ground level. The most well known of all of the pyramids is The Great Pyramid of Cheops at Giza. It is the only pyramid in Egypt where chambers have been discovered above ground level. It is famous for the King's and Queen's chambers and not so well know for its Subterranean Chamber which is 600 feet directly beneath the apex of the pyramid. Right next to the Great Pyramid is the grand Pyramid of Chephren in which a subterranean chamber is found. Interestingly enough, a ground level chamber also exists here which is directly in line with the pyramid's apex. The smaller of the three Giza pyramids is the Pyramid of Mycerinus which houses three underground chambers. To date, archeologists and Egyptologists have not been able to discern why all of the pyramids (with the exception of the Great Pyramid) have only ground level or underground compartments. Indulge me as I explain my thoughts and theory on this matter.

The ancient wise ones were obviously involved with potentizing the earth with spiritualized substance channeled through the perfected geometric structures of the pyramids. They knew that in order to actualize cosmic energy into the roots of the earth it was necessary to have the chambers exist either on the surface of the earth or beneath it. Advanced technology, greater than the world has since known, was used to channel stellar frequencies through the pyramids, connecting the cosmic grid into this planet's material substance. That technology was lost as the earth entered into its natural growth cycle and the transpersonal chakras became dormant.

What is exciting, is that now, human-light beings are capable of using their own physical vehicles to achieve the same end! The simultaneous activation of the three transpersonal chakras with the Earth Star is the key through which the cosmic forces unite with the conscious beings of the earth. We are capable of aligning ourselves with the stellar rays and grounding that essence through the Earth Star, just as the ground level and subterranean chambers in the pyramids were. If inanimate objects can accomplish such a feat, we most assuredly can as well! We have the means and the way, the choice and the will, to bring about the greatest achievement this world has ever known.

The integration of spirit into matter is dependent upon the Earth Star functioning at full capacity. When all of the chakras are harmoniously aligned and integrated with one another, new matter will literally be created. As cosmic frequencies infiltrate through us into the roots of the earth, the atoms comprising the physical plane will vibrate at a higher octave. Exactly what this means and how it will eventually manifest on this planet we can only begin to imagine. What is important is that it is possible! Each one of us has the opportunity to re-create not only our own beings, but through that, the material substance of the earth. This is the essence of The Crystalline Transmission!

Fear is all that stands in the way. Over-identification with the limited linear laws and ways of the earth has created in humankind a deeply ingrained fear of the unknown, of the dark, and of the eventual death of the physical body. If the Divine Essence is to be firmly planted into the roots of the earth it is mandatory that these fears be eliminated. Why else would the ancient ones also create the symbolic representation of the Sphinx right next to the greatest pyramids of the world? Perhaps to show us, in later days, that it is only through the elevation of our lower emotions and animal instincts that divine consciousness can be attained. The sphinx symbolizes the animal nature of the lion governed by higher consciousness of the God-man (or woman as the case may be). If it was possible thousands of years ago, it is possible now.

Be prepared in the activation of the Earth Star to undergo a transmutation of primal fears. Be ready to superimpose the

41

consciousness of the upper chakras into and through these animalistic tendencies. Stand firmly upon the earth in willingness to transform fear into higher knowing and let go of anything less than the ultimate truth. Be fortified with the understanding that all things of the physical world are destined to change and pass away and only the Divine Essence stands true in the test of time and space. Know that in reality YOU are that essence. Affirm and reaffirm your readiness to live in accordance with the principles of harmony and unconditional love that govern the way of the divine. Let everything else surrender unto that. Be prepared to live (and if necessary die) for the spiritual values and moral ethics that you know in the core of your being to be true. With that, primal fears are dissolved, the Earth Star can be activated, and a new reality commences.

Specific practices with the Sun Meditations (pages 46-49) as well as attunement and work with Hematite (Predominate Power Stone Section, pages 103-111) can be extremely helpful in strengthening the human-light being in preparation for maximum stimulation of the Earth Star Chakra.

CHAPTER III
INTEGRATING
THE CRYSTALLINE ESSENCE

Within the center core of each being lies that indefinable presence of the divine. That force animates creation with an infinite variety of forms and creatures. The greatest achievement that human beings can attain is to consciously identify with and 'become' that miraculous Crystalline Essence in living breathing form. The full activation and harmonious integration of all the twelve chakras is essential if this giant step in evolution is to occur. Of course, it will take time and effort. But, what could possibly be more important than to secure for ourselves peace of mind and a joyous heart? A little time taken each day and devoted to this process will most assuredly reap a bountiful harvest.

We are blessed to have daily access to an incredible source of light through our sun. These emanations can be consciously assimilated and used to activate our own inner Crystalline Essence. The awakening of the three transpersonal chakras is dependent upon stellar rays being converted into solar (soular) energy and integrated into the human mechanism. Our sun automatically converts cosmic energy into light and can be a great teacher for us as we learn to do the same. The Crystalline Transmission becomes a reality when we learn to synthesize light; and what better source of light do we have than that of our own parent star?

THE GLORY OF THE SUN

Throughout history mankind has worshipped the sun. For thousands of years prior to the establishment of organized religion, men and women bowed in homage to the life-producing energy radiating from the sun. The oldest known capital in Egypt was the sacred city of On, where Aton — the Disk — was worshipped as the Sun-god Ra. The city was later renamed by the Greeks and called Heliopolis meaning "City of the Sun. " The priests and priestesses of On were thoroughly versed in the wisdom of the Ancient Ones (previously referred to) and devoted their lives to the solar orb. In India, certain hymns of the Rig-Veda make distinct reference to the vedic Sun-god named Surya. One of the tenets of the Hindu religion is based upon the rotation of the solar system around the great central sun, with that great cycle of time divided into four 'yugas. ' In Peru, great sun disks were once made out of gold in honor of the God of the Inca, "Who lives forever in the sky." The ancient cultures studied and practiced astronomy and astrology with accurate proficiency. Stonehenge in England as well as Mayan and Incan astrological observatories stand witness unto this day of the fact that the motion of light held great significance to our ancestors. Solstice and equinox rituals and ceremonies are as old as history itself. Virtually every land in times of antiquity had a sun-god and separate cultures and nations independently built elaborate temples to exalt and praise the life-giving light of the sun.

Why was the sun so adored? What did the masters of old know that we have long since forgotten? Why did they attune to the sun and what powers did they attain by doing so? Of course with a little rational logic it is easy to discern that without the light and heat of the sun, the earth would be a lifeless, frozen planet. However, today in the twentieth century, industrialization, commercialism, and computerized technology reign supreme. Along with the dominance of conventional religions, worship of the sun is virtually non-existent. The majority of people on the planet live in the polluted atmospheres of large cities, where it is often difficult to even see the full radiance of the sun. For the most part, we tend to take for granted the one constant presence in our lives. We know that the sun will rise and set each day, providing the earth and all living things upon it with enlivening rays. And why would we even be so inclined to raise our arms and open our palms to glorify the sun? What benefits could be expected, what purpose does it have?

There is so much more we have yet to learn. In the stress producing, high paced, material achievement oriented society of the Western World it is often difficult to relate to simplistic truths. We complicate and compartmentalize our minds to the degree where the pure and natural things in life frequently go unnoticed. The Sun is the greatest of our teachers. It is not only the source of light and life for this planet, but through observation of its nature we can learn the essence of spirituality.

The sun is the source of nourishment for all living things upon this earth. The sun knows no prejudice or biased judgment as it sheds energy, light,and warmth upon all creatures, great or small. This unconditional love given equally to all things signifies the unity and brotherhood of all life. Man is not greater than the plants that turn their leaves to follow the sun, or the frogs that bask in the warming rays, or the fish that swim to the surface of the water to peer into the world of light. All living things upon this earth share this common source of life sustenance. The only difference lies in the fact that human consciousness is capable of identifying with the one Impersonal God, the essence of all existence, personified in the Creator of all life upon our earth, the Sun.

There is more. The sun is both spiritual light and material form, the purest manifestation of the oneness of that which is visible with the invisible, of matter and energy. The sun is deified cosmic energy, so are crystals, and potentially, so are we. The true worship of the sun is based upon attunement not only to the light, but to the ultimate essence of all existence; the force behind the force, the impersonal energy of the cosmos. The sun is the light body of the earth, just as our light bodies exist in the Soul Star region above the tops of our heads. There are billions of suns, just as there are billions of people. The fact remains that the animating force behind it all, is Divine Presence. That essence can be attuned to and integrated into our twelve chakra system by practicing the ancient common worship of the sun.

THE SUN MEDITATIONS

The Sun Meditations were originally a practice that was reserved for only the priests and priestesses, and select initiates. It is a powerful practice that should be performed only by those who are consciously participating in the Crystalline Transmission. The reason for this is that these meditations activate the three upper chakras as well as ground that energy into the Earth Star, and utmost awareness must be exercised in this process. It is recommended that you start with one meditation every seven days and gradually build your tolerance as you integrate those energies throughout the week. In practicing the Sun Meditations for over two years now, I am only able to perform them three to four times a week, at the most. Take the time that you need in-between meditations, however long it may be, until you feel the longing within your heart to again relate directly to the soul of the sun. Increase the frequency of the meditations according to the degree that you can synthesize the light harmoniously throughout your chakra system.

The Sun Meditations are to be performed only as follows. Fifteen minutes before sunrise or sunset stand with your feet firmly planted on the ground and face the sun (preferably with bare feet on the ground). This is indeed a magical time when the light rays bend creating magnificent colors that can be assimilated into the auric field. Breath long and deep, at first with your eyes closed. Begin by focussing all of your attention at the Earth Star, six inches below the soles of your feet. (If you choose, you can place Hematite at the soles of your feet to assist in activating the Earth Star). As you deeply inhale, draw the energy from below the earth into your feet and up through the back of the legs to meet at the base of the spine. Continuing with the inhale, feel that energy rise up the spine, through the top of the head and out to greet the Stellar Gateway. Hold the breath for a moment at the Stellar Chakra and then slowing begin to exhale as the energy is channeled back into the head, down the center front of the body, through the legs and feet to reconverge again at the Earth Star. Visualize the energy moving in golden beams throughout the chakra system as the gold-colored rays of the Great Central Sun are infused into the fiber of your being. Continue breathing in this circular fashion for eight to ten minutes as the frequencies of the Earth Star make a profound acquaintance with the transpersonal chakras.

The Crystalline Transmission

While breathing, raise the arms to a sixty degree angle with the palms facing toward the sun. Try to keep the arms straight and allow solar energy to enter into your palms and channel down through the arms into your heart chakra. The energy centers in the palms of the hands are stimulated in this way, increasing the healing power that can be transmitted through the hands. Do not continue with the next part of this meditation until this orbit of the breath has been well established. Until then, continue to breathe with eyes closed and the arms reaching for the sky until just after the sun has set or right before it rises. Then open the eyes, lower the arms and allow your aura to absorb the light rays while you enjoy the beauty of dawn or dusk.

When the breath orbit has been established the eyes may be opened and the gaze focussed directly into the center of the sun. DO NOT look straight into the sun three to five minutes before it sets or after it rises. This could severely damage the eyes. During the few minutes before the sun actually sets or after it has risen on the horizon, one may stare directly into it and receive stellar-solar transmissions. If the sun is rising or setting over mountains it will still probably be too high in the sky to safely look directly into. If you find that this creates eye strain or excess squinting, close your eyes and wait a minute or two before trying again. It may be that at first you only look into the sun for one minute right before it sets or after it rises. Gradually build your endurance but never exceed the five minute maximum eye contact with the sun.

As this powerful tantric connection is made with the sun, continue the circulating breath as the Earth Star and the Stellar Gate polarize one another. When these two energy centers come into alignment, the rest of the chakras will make the necessary adjustments to harmonize between these two poles. With the eyes focussed at the center of the fiery disk several alterations in the consciousness can be anticipated. First, the rotation of the earth and it's intimate association with the sun can be felt. Then, if concentrated focus is maintained, alignment is made with the sun behind our sun and a personal relationship with the Great Central Sun is established. If internal silence is sustained it is possible for the consciousness to travel through the sun, into the Great Central Sun and become one with the essence of all that is.

As the sun sinks below the horizon continue to circulate the grounding energies of the Earth Star as you escort your awareness back into your physical body. Throughout the entire meditation, especially when experiencing solar travel, keep the orbit of the breath circulating and if need be, refocus attention at the Earth Star upon completion to ensure proper grounding. To close this meditation, bring the palms together at the center of the chest and witness the glory of creation while nourishing yourself in the astounding beauty of the sky's colorful array of light.

The Sun Meditations can be practiced every day only if full integration of the stellar-solar energy is taking place and you feel your spiritual essence is being grounded and expressed in all aspects of your daily life. In the mean time, the circulating breath exercises can be performed individually on a regular basis to keep the chakra system clear and united.

The sun is a gateway of light, an opening in the universe to other dimensions, to greater galactic spheres. The Sun Meditations are one way of integrating the Divine Essence into our beings. When the human consciousness relates to the soul of the sun, to the light body of our earth, to the Great Central Sun nurturing our tiny star, and to the cosmic force beyond it all, the Crystalline Essence is experienced and shines through.

THE TRANSMISSION

As the soul of the sun is acknowledged and assimilated two things simultaneously occur. First, our own higher chakras are activated. But, as they are, we become capable of literally channeling those cosmic rays through our bodies and onto the earth. As our light bodies are integrated with our physical bodies, Terra's (the earth's) light body, which is the sun, is intricately linked into the world's material substance. The key is this: it happens through us, through the life forms upon her surface that have the capabilities to experience oneness. The manifestations that occur upon our earth are a result of our collective consciousness. If enough people transmit divine presence through their beings, transmutation and transformation will occur on a global scale. It is up to us, the ones who can relate on those levels, to commit to and prioritize this reality. As we do, others will sense the change and in subtle or overt ways will be affected by the Crystalline Transmission.

Our activated Crystalline Essence will create an aura that transmits peace and harmony. This frequency will emanate from us wherever we are and into all of the various circumstances and situations that we contend with in life. It will change the nature of how we relate to all the people that we interact with as auras mix and that cosmic frequency is subtly exchanged. It doesn't matter if we or the people that surround us are aware of it or not. We may just be filling up the tank at the gas station or doing the grocery shopping. The fact is that energy exchanges are taking place and light is being transmitted from us and going out to someone else. Or, we may choose to consciously send that love forth, to project it for another person's benefit. The important thing to remember in consciously projecting this energy out is not to define its purpose or outcome in another's life. Just send it and let the wisdom of the divine do with it whatever it will. In other words, it is not for us to define or try to control the way in which this miraculous force will go to work in someone else's life. Just send it, let go, and let God.

True healing results when the Divine Essence is transmitted. It will not be limited to just interpersonal relationships, even though that's where the change starts. Watch it as is starts to transform the business and political worlds. Modalities will begin to alter and come into harmony with the all pervading force. In that process, also be prepared for great change and hold true to your inner knowing. Do not compromise spiritual values and principles. Lean on the trust that you, within the sacred sanctums of your innermost being, know to be true. Yes, it may yet be a hundred years before the Crystalline Transmission sprouts into all of the world's affairs. It may take even longer. This is truly the greatest transition the human race has ever known and you are an intregal and vital part of it. Plant the seeds now that the children of the future will harvest. What an exciting time to be alive! Let's make the absolute most of it. Who knows, you may reappear in the not too distant future to take part in the bounty of the crystalline seeds that you sow today!

SECTION II

THE PREDOMINANT
POWER STONES

INTRODUCTION TO THE
PREDOMINANT POWER STONES

Selenite, Kyanite, Calcite, and Hematite are the Predominant Power Stones, each serving a significant function in the Crystalline Transmission. It is no accident that these stones are being activated at this time as we, as a race, embark upon the most exciting and fulfilling phase yet of our evolutionary growth process. These Predominant Power Stones are the very tools needed to assist us in grounding our light bodies into our physical bodies and transforming the possibilities of peace and harmony into living realities. With their assistance the process of infiltrating the earth with light is accelerated and the dissemination of spirit into matter is further advanced. Working with the energies transmitted through these stones the veils in our consciousness can be lifted, atomic frequencies elevated, genetic codings altered and conscious connection to our source stabilized.

The Crystalline Transmission

Each of the crystalline entities discussed in this section come fully equipped and prepared to relay and transmit certain pertinent knowledge and energies into our beings. Together they work as a very powerful team to fully integrate the infinite spirit force into every aspect of our minds, hearts, bodies and souls. Selenite is at the helm, activating the light body through the Soul Star above the top of the head. Kyanite then takes over to usher that energy into the highest levels of the mind to be used in the conscious creation of thought. Calcite integrates and blends Selenite's clear white light with all other aspects of the self as it bridges the essence of the new with the harvest of lifetimes of lessons. Hematite, in its brilliance of the earth, will ground the light force into the soles of our feet with such grace and strength that we will bow in reverence and in gratitude to the blessings that have blossomed from physical incarnation. In so doing, the Earth Star below the soles of the feet will be activated and all that is possible in the realm of spirit will be likewise seen and experienced upon the earth.

To aid in this process a specialized advanced layout is shared at the end of this section after a complete portrayal of each stone is given. However, please be aware that it may take years of preparation before the Advanced Initiation Layout using the Predominant Power Stones can be successfully performed. The practice of this layout is not to be taken lightly or to be used without proper preparation, guidance and/or assistance from a trained Crystal Healer. In the meantime, attunement, meditation and work with these stones will serve to open the channels and clear the way for the Crystalline Transmission to be a growing reality in your life.

It is my pleasure to present to you The Predominant Power Stones that have come to serve in our transformation during the 1990's. What an incredibly special time we live in right now! What a blessing and honor it is to be alive as the earth makes her deserved passage into wholeness and union.

Introduction To The Predominant Power Stones

You are a vital aspect of that transition and serve a very special purpose in the changes that will take place in the next decade. Do not underestimate the power of the part you play. As you find more peace in your heart of hearts and integrate the light of your Soul Star with your Earth Star, this planet will receive your transmission and be healed by it. What more can any of us do than to come to peace with ourselves? The Predominant Power Stones are here to serve us in that process by activating, integrating, balancing and grounding. May your experience with them be as transformative as mine was.

CHAPTER IV

SELENITE

Before writing this chapter on Selenite I researched my left brain resource books to try to gain some intellectual information that would give me clues about its nature. I could find only scanty, if any, reference directly to Selenite and was referred to general information on Gypsum, of which Selenite is a variety. Obviously, much of what there was to know about Selenite had not yet been written or known to date. This was no great surprise since Selenite is one of the crystalline forms that has just recently been activated and is only now beginning to reveal itself. I would like to share a personal experience that I had with Selenite which taught me more than any written information ever could.

Some time ago I received two large boxes of Selenite crystals, which under normal circumstances would have been picked up by my co-workers and taken to the Crystal Academy. Instead they were picked up by my partner and brought directly to my office at home where I have been writing this book. As I unwrapped them I was very pleased when I saw such fine Selenite crystals. I immediately noticed that two of the crystals were bent and curved.

Since I was just beginning to write about Selenite I knew it was no accident that the crystals were brought to my home to assist with the new information that would be written about them. The next day, as I cleansed my writing altar and prepared myself to resonate with Selenite in order to receive its knowledge I felt excited, like something special was going to happen. I attributed it to the fact that 'Master Selenite' was getting ready to speak. I then went to the crystals that I had received in order to place some of them on my altar, create a Selenite grid, and surround myself with them. As I unwrapped the crystals again I was astonished by the phenomenon that I witnessed. Instead of just two bent Selenite crystals, eleven out of nineteen were curved instead of straight. Some were even bending in front of my eyes. It was obvious that Selenite was definitely trying to relay something very important.

It was evident to me, as I sat and watched the Selenite crystals continue to change shape before my very eyes, that this crystal is endowed with a special ability to alter the very nature of physical matter. Yes, I know that the skeptics will say "prove it!" What more proof do we need than that which is witnessed with our very eyes and acknowledged with the essence of our beings? Perhaps that is what Selenite is trying to say here; that the world of form and matter is adjustable, that what we perceive to be material reality is in fact able to change and alter itself. The laws that govern the physical plane are transmutable. We have accepted them as absolute, definable and oh, so very rational because they are able to be proven with the linear frame of thinking. But, what happens to our reality when we see, understand and know that those laws are governed by yet greater laws? What would happen if we attuned ourselves to that frame of comprehension and decided instead to work with those principles of reality?

Is it not true that 'as one believeth, so it is'? We no longer need to be bound by the beliefs that the spirit cannot move freely in the physical world and that in order to go to heaven we first have to die and leave our bodies. We no longer need to accept anything less than that which is proven to be real from within our own knowingness. That is the statement that Selenite makes and what it has demonstrated. All things are possible here on the earth. Not only does Selenite prove that, it will teach us how to incorporate those divine laws and principles of being into our earthly reality.

In the Golden Age, which we are rapidly approaching, light will become one with the physical world. Selenite is very much like a harbinger to this age of enlightenment as it heralds the approach of the marriage between spirit and matter. Presently we are limited to governing our reality with only the material laws which are very much bound to the illusionary nature of time and space. But, as the dawn of the coming age grows brighter upon the horizon, we will come to understand the lessons that Selenite is transmitting. Essentially, we will be capable ourselves, of integrating into our physical structures the light force that has always been representative of spirit. Then, the laws of light will govern the ways of the world and reality will shift to include infinite possibilities while inhabiting a physical body.

It has been an honor to witness and experience Selenite transform itself in this way. I send this transmission to you now so that as you read, you too, can receive this incredible Selenite energy. If you have any Selenite of your own why don't you get it out and have it near you as you read this so that you can better attune to and personally partake in its energy. Don't be surprised if as you do, it bends and curls to let you know that it's more alive and aware than you might have ever guessed!

THE NATURE OF SELENITE

New Selenite mines have recently been discovered in the Four Corners area of the United States. The Southwest is one of the awakening vortexes of the New Age where the future communities will be birthed. Selenite is preparing the way by establishing a frequency of light in the earth where new seeds of consciousness are being planted for the coming times.

As mentioned earlier, Selenite is a variety of Gypsum which is a common mineral found in sedimentary rocks. Selenite is one of the first minerals that is formed from evaporating salt water in land locked lakes or in seas isolated from the open oceans. Metaphorically speaking, we could say that Selenite is indeed a rare and wonderful 'salt of the earth.' As humans, we also contain a large amount of saline solution in our bodies. Being born out of the same ocean of life as Selenite, it stands to reason that on some primal level, we would resonate with the essence of this crystal.

Selenite manifests in ice clear, striated, fine, delicate crystals. It can terminate either in the v-shape commonly known as twinning, in a 'fish-tail' configuration, or in a single extended point. Selenite is an extremely soft, fragile crystal, measuring only 2 on the Mohs' Hardness Scale. One of the distinguishing characteristics of Selenite is that it is soft enough to scratch with your fingernail. Be very gentle in handling it and be aware that if you are thinking or acting out negative thoughts it is possible that sensitive Selenite will fracture or break. Most Selenite crystals are striated which means that the long parallel protruding lines running the length of the crystal will strengthen, energize and channel high frequency energy through the body of the crystal. Selenite is like liquid light; its striations are the pathways for the illuminated substance of spirit.

Selenite resides on that thread of a threshold between pure white light and physical matter. It vibrates more on the spiritual level than that of the physical. That is one of the reasons why Selenite can bend, curl, turn red hot and back again before your very eyes. Capable of displaying total transparency, Selenite's essence is that of which dreams and visions are made. Unlike the clearest of Quartz, which can work on all levels of physicality, Selenite builds the bridge through which the highest frequencies of light can be integrated with the most subtle levels of form. Bending pure white light to manifest onto the earth plane is Selenite's forte. It then becomes the job of Kyanite, Calcite, Hematite, and a host of other crystalline entities to further channel and densify that energy into other facets of human expression.

Chemically, Selenite is hydrous calcium sulfate. The word 'hydrous' means that Selenite is bonded with water as a primary component in its makeup. The fact that Selenite is so closely related to water provides us with valuable insight concerning its nature and purpose. If we relate to the emotions as the water element, we can then imply that Selenite has a direct effect on the emotional body. But unlike stones that will soothe and calm the emotions like Smithsonite (see page 251) and Green Aventurine (see *Crystal Healing*, Vol. II, pages. 189-190), Selenite serves a unique purpose in activating that aspect of our nature that is true 'spiritual feeling.' Water bubbles are often found in Selenite wands. These crystals are particularly effective in stabilizing the emotional body and bringing erratic e-motions under calm control. Selenite is water soluble which means that it will eventually dissolve if left in liquid. This characteristic also endows Selenite with the power to melt away exaggerated e-motions with the stabilizing light force of true feeling.

FROM SOURCE TO FEELING

We are all familiar with the human pendulum of e-motion which swings from sadness to gladness, from grief to relief, from anger to contentment and from depression to elation. Generally these e-motions are felt to some degree on a daily basis as we react to the conditions that life in the world of matter will present. Yet, there exists a higher octave of our feeling nature that in most of us humans is not yet fully matured. This highly refined level of sensation occurs when the soul emanates its essence into our hearts. It is the very vibration that accompanies all spiritual experiences, revelations, intuitions, and states of unconditional love and peace of mind. But these experiences are all too often short lived and become only a faint echo in the memory of our hearts as the emotional pendulum sweeps us off center balance once again to fluctuate on the merry-go-round of the world. Selenite has now arrived on the scene and with it comes a new set of laws that when applied have the potential to assist us in shifting our over-identification with the e-motions to the higher characteristics of our spiritual-feeling nature. Because of its striations, Selenite has a unique ability to transmit the essence of higher octave spiritualized feeling into the realm of human e-motion. In so doing seemingly uncontrollable e-motional energy is alchemized as attunement is made to the Christed heart within each being.

Try holding a striated Selenite wand (preferably one with water bubbles inside) and gently stroking it next time you feel your e-motions taking over. Breathe long and deep as you inhale the Selenite energy and exhale whatever the controlling e-motion is. Continue until you feel aligned with the strength, stability and spiritualized sensations that Selenite will transmit. This meditation can be practiced daily, even when e-motions are not out of hand, in order to redefine your association with your true feelings and as a protection from over-emotionalism. In this way, Selenite helps us develop the fragile feminine essence of 'spiritual feeling' so that we can continuously respond to our heart's calling instead of reacting to the world's transient ways.

ACTIVATING THE SOUL STAR

Selenite is the crystal that can be used to activate the Soul Star (see Chapter 2, pages 29-33). The Soul Star is the energy center that is located six inches above the top of the head. Through it an individual can access the infinite source of omnipresent energy that exists at the Stellar Gateway. The Soul Star is located outside of the physical body and therefore is not bound by the laws that dominate the material realm. Once Selenite activates the Soul Star it is then possible for the light body to permeate the aura enabling this spiritualized essence to be assimilated by the crown chakra. This is an important and necessary step in the Crystalline Transmission, for it prepares the entire chakra system to disseminate the influx of light into the entire rainbow ray spectrum.

The light body is likened unto the sun, whose rays sustain all life on this planet. Just so, the light of the spirit sustains your being and provides you with the inspiration that feeds your faith and gives you the strength to continue upon life's path. For a moment, imagine what it would be like if you no longer lost sight of your spiritual identity, if you were forever aligned, attuned and one with your infinite source. This is possible now that Selenite has revealed its secrets and solved the mystery of how to bend light and adjust physical form. Selenite will transmit the teachings of illumination so that your spirit can find a cozy home in your body.

With proper use and personal preparation Selenite can assist one in creating an entirely new fabric of being here on the earth. By simultaneously elevating the frequency of physical matter and lowering the frequency of light, Selenite knows how to delicately design a new substance through which spirit can be actualized in matter. As this occurs new synapses and circuits are created enabling the light body to fully inhabit the denser levels of being. It is only a matter of time until the Selenite light transmission strengthens and transforms the nervous and endocrine systems. Finally, the blood will carry the message of the 'new way' into every living cell of the human body. As this revolutionary human advancement transpires, the blessings of the spiritual realms will descend to work miracles in your life and upon the earth.

CAUTION ABOUNDS

The use of Selenite in the Predominant Power Stone Initiation (page 113) is NOT to be underestimated or taken lightly. Many subtle and profound changes will occur on every level within each being who undergoes this type of light initiation. One must be dedicated to the ways of Spirit and be prepared to process the effects of the Selenite transfusion of light. Each person who feels the calling, who knows from within the depths of their being that it is truly time to become One with all that they potentially can be, cannot refuse such an opportunity. The Predominant Power Stone Layout (forthcoming) will provide the participant with the ways and means to use Selenite in its highest capacity. **Be sure you are prepared before-hand by becoming familiar with Selenite's frequency in your private meditations, having crystal healings, and practicing the circulating breath exercises before embarking upon such a transformative experience.**

It is of vital importance that the Earth Star, (see page 38) located six inches below the soles of the feet be activated before the Soul Star is over-stimulated. The Soul Star and the Earth Star are like soul mates, intimately connected to each other and requiring one another in order to reach completion and fulfillment. If Selenite is used above the top of the head to energize the Soul Star before the polarity base of the Earth Star has been founded, great damage can be created.

I know that there are many among you who would prefer to become One with the light at the Soul Star and not relate or identify to the earth's heartaches or to our own physical realities. From my own experience, I understand this. I also know that it is only through our commitment to healing the earth, which has been such a great source of learning and growth for us, can this planet become part of a greater galactic sphere. Only by establishing our connection into the very substance of the earth, and activating the Earth Star beneath our feet, can we bring the light of the Soul Star into the roots of the planet. In doing so, we will nourish ourselves, as well as our earth-mother Terra, back to health.

When our feet are firmly planted on the ground then the foundation can bear the transfusion of light that will be channeled in from an infinite source through the Soul Star. If however, we are not grounded and have not personally cleared and healed our own mental and emotional bodies, physical as well as ethereal damage can be created as the light is diffused and dispersed throughout the various energy systems of the human body. A great strain will be put on the nervous system and severe disorientation and disassociation can result, as well as headaches, lower back aches and vision problems. In short, it can be a set back. It is the responsibility of each person working with Selenite, whether it be on yourself or others, to simultaneously activate the Earth Star and ground Selenite's high frequency light force with stones such as Black Tourmaline, Smoky Quartz, and most importantly Hematite.

SELENITE'S MISSION

Aside from channeling spiritual feeling and activating the Soul Star, Selenite can be used in several other ways. As previously written in *Crystal Enlightenment*, Vol. I (pages 151-153), Selenite's exceptional clarity can be used to clear the mind and bring high frequency light rays into any environment. Selenite is capable of recording mystical secrets written on the rays of white light. The laws of light, encoded within the inner chambers of transparent Selenite crystals, are accessible only to those who can still and clear their own minds. Then, the unclouded mind can take a magical journey into the inner sanctums of the crystal and perceive the wisdom and knowledge recorded therein.

Selenite can also be used in thought transmission. First clear the mind and then detail a thought that you would like to relay to either another person or out into the collective mind. Then place the Selenite to the third eye and project the thought out. With the inherent powers of Selenite the thought will travel faster than the speed of light. This is a wonderful way to transmit positive thoughtforms out into the collective mind to be perceived either consciously or subconsciously by the millions of beings who are reaching towards their wholeness.

Selenite can be used in crystal healings if you use accompanying grounding stones. Black Tourmaline is a perfect polarity balance for clear Selenite as they are both striated and the white light rays are easily channeled and balanced by the grounding dark presence of Tourmaline. Hematite is also a complimentary companion and should be used on the navel, pubic bone, groin points, or feet when using Selenite above the top of the head in crystal healings. Make sure that the person that you are working with is ready to bring in more light before using Selenite. If so, have them inhale the light in through the center line to the base of their spine and exhale it through the soles of their feet to connect with the

Selenite

earth (see *Crystal Healing*, Volume II, pages 24-27). With the majority of people receiving crystal healings, the process generally involves letting go, clearing and establishing a conscious connection with their source. In these cases, Selenite is usually not used. Only when one is consciously prepared to assimilate and integrate abundant light should Selenite's energy be utilized in crystal healings.

Because Selenite connects one to the light body, it can be used under the right conditions to assist in the death process. This is of course a great responsibility that should be accompanied by very clear guidance and practiced only with the conscious participation of the dying person. In this process, a naturally terminated Selenite wand is placed above the top of the head with the termination pointing towards the Soul Star. The breath is inhaled up through the feet and exhaled out of the top of the head. Hold the breath out for a moment as concentration is held at the Soul Star. With the focus and conscious identification on the light of the Soul Star outside of the body, it is easier for a person to release physical as well as emotional attachments that make the death transition more difficult. This exercise should not be practiced for more than eleven minutes three times a day and a crystal healer should be present.

Selenite can be used at the third eye point for astral projection, though it is not advised except in situations where one is consciously developing the higher powers of the mind for positive purposes. Even then, it is very important to have a defined destination and not just beam out into the astral regions to possibly find yourself in an undesirable situation. Place a Selenite crystal at the third eye with the termination pointing outward. Inhale as you visualize energy rising up the spine to be exhaled out of the third eye as your consciousness travels out the Selenite crystal to your chosen destination. I would advise extreme caution in these circumstances as well as the assistance of a certified crystal healer and the use of a large supply of grounding stones.

The Crystalline Transmission

As I complete this section and gaze upon the Selenite crystals surrounding me, I cannot help but notice that they are now not only curved but waving. I know there is more yet to be discovered from these pure messengers of light. But, for now, what Selenite seems to be relaying is that if we work with the spiritual laws that have dominion over the physical plane then unlimited possibilities open up. When light bends, as in the wonder of sunrise or sunset, exquisite colors and magical energy can be experienced. Through my own experience with Selenite, I know now that it too has the power to bend spiritual light in order to be integrated onto the physical plane and infused into our beings. As time goes by and we become more identified with our spirits, and our light bodies become better integrated with our physical bodies, Selenite will continue to educate us in the ways of the new reality.

CHAPTER V
KYANITE

Kyanite's time has come to claim its rightful place as one of the Predominant Power Stones in the next decade. It has laid dormant for thousands of years until the cosmic clock ticked the exact right moment. Now Kyanite has awakened and its power is fully restored. Kyanite is unique in its cause and no other crystalline entity can replace its specific purpose or perform its sole function. Kyanite is destined for greatness as it serves a specialized role in our human unfoldment in the 1990's.

Our own evolution parallels the present empowerment of Kyanite. For many thousands of years we have struggled through the ages of darkness and forgetfulness. For lifetimes, it may have seemed as if we were lost. In that sense of primal abandonment the tests and trials of humanness were suffered. We have strived long and hard to gain mastery over our physical senses, our mental and emotional bodies, and the transient ways of the world. It is now possible to gather the harvest of our earthly experiences and come into alignment with the Divine Essence of our own beings. Just as with Kyanite, we are also awakening to another level of attunement, of Oneness. As with Kyanite, we too, can perform a very specialized purpose for our planet and the race of human beings that inhabit it.

KYANITE'S CHARACTERISTICS

Kyanite is a blue mineral that forms in long bladed crystals. The color is often irregular with occasional streaks of white, green, yellow or pink. Like Selenite, these long flat crystals are striated. This indicates that the parallel lines protruding along the length of the crystal will amplify and conduct high frequency electrical energies. (See *Striated Power, Crystal Healing*, Volume II, page 179). The specialized energy that Kyanite transmits through its striations is the subtle etheric essence of thought.

Kyanite varies in hardness on the Mohs' Hardness Scale from 4 to 7.5. The fact that Kyanite demonstrates such extreme variation in density provides another key to unlocking the mystery of its purpose and use. In translating the symbolic language that crystals speak, this signifies that Kyanite is able to fluctuate its frequency from etheric states of expanded consciousness into denser levels of the mind where intuition, comprehension, intellectualization and understanding can occur. Kyanite, with its fibrous adjustability, directs and channels the Divine Essence into the etheric substance of the mind to create thoughts that are capable of maintaining the primal integrity of spiritual force. This Predominant Power Stone also enables the mind to access those realms of causal thought that ultimately determine what will become manifest on the physical plane.

Kyanite

Because of Kyanite's varied hardness, it is often brittle and can be fractured and easily broken. Or, on less common occasion, it can be hard enough to cut and facet. Kyanite, in gem quality cut stones, are a wonder to behold and make wonderful contributions to a collection of healing stones. In the long bladed form, Kyanite serves yet another powerful purpose which will be discussed shortly.

It is also interesting to note that Kyanite forms in the Triclinic System, which has the least symmetry of any of the geometric crystal systems. None of the axes are at right angles to each other. When deciphering Kyanite's symbolism, this implies that it is less related to the physical plane than many other crystals or stones. If we associate the materiality of the third dimension to a cube, we find that it is solely comprised of right angles, bringing into form height, width, and depth, i.e. time and space. With Kyanite, we are working with another set of laws altogether; laws that are able to conform to cubical realities but are in no way bound or ruled by them. The adaptability of symmetry endows Kyanite with the power to usher elevated frequencies into the cubical box of the mind and in so doing, human mentality is transformed.

FROM ORIGIN TO COGNITION

The causal level is the highest and most subtle aspect of what we define as 'mind.' It is in that realm where the all pervasive frequency of spiritual force initially actualizes into thought forms. Kyanite's intent and purpose is to connect the lines of energy from the light body into that causal realm of the etheric mind. As it does, the Causal Chakra is activated and the laws of light, which give birth to unlimited possibilities, can be conceived and incorporated into all of our thinking modes. Then, the Divine Essence will be empowered to adjust the thinking patterns to accommodate higher frequency thought forms that are attuned to the Soul Star and the Stellar Gateway. Maintaining alignment with these two highest chakras, spiritual integrity is maintained in the newly formed thoughts that will blossom into advanced concepts, beliefs and ideologies.

The mind is the blueprint for what will manifest materially. By establishing and integrating the light body into the mental plane with Kyanite, new synapses are created through which the light of the soul can permanently reside in the mind. With the thoughts determined by the spiritual energies emanating from the Soul Star and The Stellar Gateway, dreams and visions can take physical form in our daily lives. Kyanite initiates new powers of manifestation as it rejuvenates the higher powers of the mind that have laid dormant for thousands of years. With dedicated use of Kyanite, the vision that has been carried in the soul's memory of 'the garden' will be remembered and resurrected. Our thoughts will gain the power to transport our beings where ever we wish to go without traversing through time or space. Everything that was possible in the days of The Ancients will be proven and implemented into a new society. Most importantly, each soul will gain constant conscious access to the source that unites all of creation. With that as a foundation, inconceivable harmony and peace can prevail, within as well as externally.

Kyanite is the builder of the very important bridge that will unite the light body to the physical via the mind. Kyanite's mission is best achieved if it is worked with in conjunction with Selenite, to activate the light body, and green or black Tourmaline to then transmit that energy into the physical nervous system. With this powerful trinity of striated stones the necessary links are made that will channel the pure spirit light force (Selenite) into the mind (Kyanite) and then into the physical body (Tourmaline). All three of these synapses are necessary if we are to truly live to our potential and utilize the wonders of the spirit in our thoughts and material creations.

KYANITE PRACTICES

There are several ways in which this Predominant Power Stone can be used outside of the Predominant Power Stone Layout and the Kyanite Infusion (page 78). As with any power stone, it is always advisable to spend quiet meditation time with the crystal to gain personal attunement before embarking on advanced practices with yourself or others. Place it to your heart, third eye and at the Causal Chakra center in personal meditations. Be open to any impressions or guidance that you may receive from the crystal that will assist you in future work with it. It may also relay to your knowing other prohibitory practices that would further ready you for the full Kyanite infusion and the Predominant Power Stone Layout.

Kyanite also serves another specialized function in opening the lines of energy in initial Earthkeeper activation (see *Crystal Healing*, Volume II, pages 155-164). In recent participation of such an event, at the Church Of San Marga on the Island of Kauai where one of the Earthkeepers has been enshrined, I was guided to use a Kyanite wand. Holding a sharp Kyanite blade three inches away from the huge crystal, I aurically traced all of the lines and angles of the Earth-keeper. It was obvious that Kyanite was catalyzing the beginning phases of activation by extending the energy around the Earthkeeper so that the crystal's innate power could be released. The Kyanite blade increased the Earth-keeper's forcefield in order to bring further transformation to those who came around it. This process in the initial phase of activation would in turn prepare The Earthkeeper for intermediate stages of activation. This type of Kyanite outlining procedure can also be used on other crystals. Before doing this however, always attune to the crystal and make sure that it wants to have its lines of energy open and its forcefield extended.

Like the Laser Wands, Kyanite blades, if sharp and pointed at the end, have the power to make incisions in the auric field. Potentially, they can cut through layers of mental misconceptions and create new lines of energy through which virgin thought can flow. If empowered by the user with conscious intention, the Kyanite blades can establish an etheric blueprint as it stabilizes the physical mind-brain with spiritual substance.

In advanced crystal healing practices sharp Kyanite blades can be used to define, outline and open new etheric spaces. When practicing this type of refined procedure be sure that the recipient is ready and prepared to let go of unneeded and unnecessary thought forms and receive an expanded perspective. This type of layout can also be used to clarify and define visions or prophetic dreams. To perform, follow the therapeutic procedures in *Crystal Healing*, Volume II, Part I and place stones on the body accordingly. Then, place a clear Selenite wand eight inches above the top of the head with the termination pointing towards the crown, and a Black Tourmaline between the feet with the termination pointing towards a triangle of three large Hematite stones six inches below the feet. It is also beneficial in this layout to use several Green, Dark Green, or Black Tourmaline pieces running from the groin points all the way down the legs. Hematite can also be placed in the hands as well as at the navel and center of the pubic bone. Once deep complete breathing and internalized focus have been established, place a Kyanite blade between the Selenite and the crown chakra, with the point of the Kyanite touching the Causal Chakra point. When the Kyanite is in place, work with the recipient to receive, clarify and define the subtle impressions that he/ she receives. Of course, a strong maintenance plan would most assuredly follow this type of advanced crystal healing practice to help integrate the energy and stabilize brain wave patterns. (See Maintenance Plan, pgs. 87-93, *Crystal Healing*, Vol. II).

Kyanite is one of the most effective crystals to use in the process of opening and clearing the subtle energy pathways of the body. Prepared with a thorough knowledge of Acupressure or Acupuncture, it can be directly used on the meridian points to stimulate the flow of energy in the body. Kyanite can be used by trained crystal healers to clear energy blockages in the chakra centers or anywhere along the center line. Kyanite is best utilized in conjunction with the other crystals and stones in this category — Selenite, Hematite and Calcite. Combined with a dedicated practice of the circulating breath exercises (see pages 47-48) and with proper guidance, Kyanite can be a wonderful assistant in defining and opening up the new circuits of energy in preparation for the Crystalline Transmission.

Kyanite is also a good friend to the new breed of beings that are now incarnating onto the earth as well as with souls who are striving to integrate material realities with the higher frequency energies that are prevalent everywhere on the planet today. Kyanite can be carried or worn by members of these soul groups to facilitate the assimilation of cosmic rays into their daily lives. It can be placed next to newly born infants to assist in their grounding process. It can also be used in conjunction with Moldavite Tektite (see pages 241-245) to assist in imbalances that may occur within the brains of newly incarnating souls as they strive to adjust to lower brain wave frequencies and assimilate physical reality. Used in crystal healings in conjunction with Elestials, Green Tourmaline and Moldavite Tektite, Kyanite will assist in creating new lines of energy to connect the light source to the mind for those who are suffering with epilepsy, autism, stroke symptoms and other forms of brain-mind imbalances.

Finally, this multi-purpose stone can be used lengthwise in the aura to smooth out the the electro-magnetic field as accelerated growth and transformation occurs. After a crystal healing, or when in need of calming, hold a long Kyanite blade lengthwise six inches above the body. In smooth long strokes, run the blade from the top of the head all the way down to the toes, until all of the space in the aura has been sufficiently covered. The recipient can be lying down, but standing is preferable as it enables the aura in the front as well as the back and the sides of the body to be stroked. Afterwards, have the recipient take several long deep circulating breaths to consolidate and integrate the effects.

THE KYANITE INFUSION

The Kyanite Infusion is performed in the Predominant Power Stone Layout (given at the end of this section). Kyanite's purpose in this Initiation is to usher the pure white light existing at the Soul Star into causal levels of the mind. Through its etheric blue striated pathways, Kyanite opens the entrance gate at the Causal Chakra and initiates the mind with pure spirit force. As the Causal Chakra is activated in this way, new thought forms are created that are empowered with Divine Essence. As with all things in the realm of matter, it will take time and effort for these new thought waves to manifest in a fresh mental outlook. Kyanite can be further utilized in a strong maintenance plan following this layout to keep the mind open to divine impressions. It can be held at the third eye or in the palm of the hand in meditation to secure the mental blueprint that is destined to manifest in wondrous form.

One must be prepared and consciously aware in the process of a Kyanite Infusion. This powerful process will have a direct effect upon the subtle energy channels of the body including the meridian and chakra systems, as well as the mind. Before this advanced crystal work is performed, it is vitally important that the recipient as well as the healer be prepared and purified on physical, mental and emotional levels. This is very important in order to prepare the mind, subtle energy pathways, and the nervous system for the accelerated energy that will flow once the Causal Chakra is activated. (Specific preparatory requirements are in Chapter 8). When both the receiver and the administrator are adequately prepared the Kyanite Infusion and the Advanced Layout can be performed. This infusion of spirit into the mind will transform the nature of your thoughts in a way that will effect your life forever.

CHAPTER VI

CALCITE

Calcite warrants much more acknowledgment and attention than what has been previously written in *Crystal Healing*, Vol. II, see pages 181, and 190-192). As a Predominant Power Stone, Calcite can be a close and dear friend in these rapidly accelerated and changing times. One of the most important lessons Calcite relays is the 'art of being.' If one tries to grasp Calcite's secrets with just the mind, its true significance can not be embraced. The training is rather to allow your "Being" to perceive the Calcite impressions and spontaneously assimilate the essence of its teaching. The 'know'ledge that Calcite has to offer extends far beyond linear mental association and into the realm of true 'knowing.' My advice in your practice and attunement to this crystal is to simply 'BE' with it. Just allow yourself to become clear and open in order to receive the multi-dimensional transmissions of light and 'know'-ledge that can't help but alter the way in which you perceive reality.

Calcite manifests in a rainbow ray of expression as does Tourmaline and Quartz. Whenever a mineral has the capacity to reflect a variety of color frequency it is evident that the crystal also has the ability to serve many functions as it synchronizes its energy to the color vibrations of the different chakras. Calcite is most commonly found in pink, peach, orange, green, clear, yellow (citrine) and gold (honey) but can also be blue, black, grey and red (usually resulting from growth with other minerals). It manifests in varying degrees of transparency and luster, from optically clear to opaque.

Like Selenite, Calcite is formed in water. Demonstrating its extreme versatility, Calcite crystallizes into over 700 varieties of form. The two major types and most well known forms of Calcite are the rhomboid shaped crystals and the terminated points commonly known as "dogtooth." Calcite is calcium carbonate and is a very soft, susceptible mineral. It should be treated with great care. It is sensitive to heat, water and sun and will easily cleave, break or chip if roughly handled. In many ways Calcite is like a new born star-child who is just getting acclimated to the earth and must be treated with attuned and sensitive care or it is liable to fall apart. But, when properly looked after and aligned with, many wonders can be revealed!

A MIRROR TO HARMONIC PERFECTION

If you were to accidentally drop a rhomboid shaped piece of Calcite, all of the fragmented pieces would break into rhomboid forms, i.e. all of the broken parts would have flat parallel sided faces. Please, you can take my word for it and save your Calcite for greater purposes than this type of experimentation! Instead, just observe a piece of Calcite that has been chipped and notice the fragment and/or where the missing

THE PREDOMINANT POWER STONES

Center: Selenite and Kyanite
Bottom Left to Rt: Stellar Beam Calcite, Rhomboid Calcite with Hematite

piece has been broken off. You will find that the area as well as the chip are also rhomboid in shape. If one of the broken pieces were further broken, the new pieces would also perfectly represent the original rhomboid form. This significantly exemplifies that crystals are made up of tiny identical basic building blocks that when stacked together comprise the complete physical crystal that can be experienced with the senses. In other words, on the atomical level, the atoms are forming together in microscopic rhomboid shapes. This primal geometric shape continues to manifest into the beautiful Calcite crystal that you can hold in your hand. This basic unity of Calcite's atomical patterning is repeated endlessly throughout the body of the crystal, teaching us one of the natural laws of the universe; that a whole exists within a whole, the smallest unit representing the largest and comprising the foundation for structures of grandeur.

Calcite clearly demonstrates the atomical synchronicity with which all highly evolved crystalline structures will manifest. It is as if one of the purposes of Calcite is to prove to our senses that there is a profound order in the universe. Because Calcite so obviously maintains its primal structure and symmetry, it becomes possible for us to perceive a divine truth. When the pure cosmic force comes into material form, and in this case into the perfect geometric form of Calcite, it is possible to maintain that integrity of balance, unity and harmony throughout all different levels and realms of manifestation.

The natural softness of Calcite and its vulnerability to cleave is another symbolic lesson. This in and of itself demonstrates how unattached Calcite is to any one physical form. It is almost as if it knows that no matter what happens to it or how small it gets, it loses nothing because its primal integrity of spiritual force is maintained. Calcite clearly represents the reality of 'a whole existing within a whole' and the multi-dimensional perfection of the universe.

Calcite

LINKING PARALLEL REALITIES

Calcite, in the rhomboid form displays six parallel planes, all connected together by one another. Each of the six four-sided parallelograms exist in their own unique plane of reality, yet each is intricately attached to four of the other parallel sides by sharing one of the angles in common. Calcite demonstrates a rare statement of order as the harmonious integration of identical geometric structures unite in one crystal.

When looking straight on at one of the parallelograms comprising Calcite, we see two horizontal parallel lines at the top and bottom joined together by two vertical parallel lines. In allowing ourselves to just 'BE, ' the obvious message of parallel realities can be impressed upon the consciousness and an entire world of new understanding can blossom forth. Each line represents a linear reality existing individually, yet we are faced with the whole geometric form which links each line intricately to the next. Hence, these Calcite crystals in the rhomboid form are the best tools around to assist us in linking parallel realities.

The term "parallel reality" can have different meanings. There are three main ways that the rhomboid Calcite crystals can teach us how to link seemingly totally separate realities.

Bringing Spirit Into Matter

The most common use Calcite serves in linking parallel realities is that of creating a conscious bridge of spiritual understanding into circumstances or situations that are challenging here on the earth plane. Calcite greatly assists in gaining insight into why certain circumstances in life have been attracted and what the spiritual significance and soul-level lessons are. In cases when you cannot see your way out of a cycle or pattern, or when you become so immersed in the physical plane reality that your consciousness fails to see divine meaning, use Calcite crystals. They will help integrate the spiritual reality into whatever situation is at hand. With this insight, it becomes much easier to accept the responsibility to learn the true lessons involved in life's experiences.

Working with Calcite in this way enables the mind to perceive alternative choices, possibilities and solutions which otherwise might elude the consciousness. Calcite's innate ability to harmoniously bridge together, assists in creating an understanding of just how the spiritual reality is intricately interwoven with all manifestations on the material plane. Not only does it bridge the physical with the spiritual, it actually assists in merging the two realities together as one by dissolving the illusion of separation.

To use Calcite for this purpose a specific meditation proves worthwhile. Hold a piece of clear Calcite level with your face and allow your sight to become focused at the very center point of the crystal. Envision the upper parallel line to be the divine spiritual purpose behind all earthly events. See the bottom parallel line to be the physical plane reality which is presenting the challenge in your life. Know that the crystalline impression of the parallelogram will serve to connect the two realities within your own being. As you gaze into the center of the crystal allow the peace of simply "being" to embrace you. Be sensitive to any impressions that you will receive within your heart or your mind's eye that will give you insight into the predicament at hand. Hold the crystal steady as you focus for at least eleven minutes (the perfect number to put perception onto a new level) while the Calcite transmits parallel perfection into your aura. When finished close your eyes and sit in silence while you integrate and assimilate Calcite's transmission.

This type of meditation, if done every day with dedication, can have profound effects upon your understanding. It will also greatly serve in your ability to make necessary changes in your attitudes, behavior and life-style in order to encompass a greater reality. It is important when practicing this meditation to not expect complete enlightenment and transformation the first time. The changes may be subtle and barely noticeable at first but are guaranteed to bring greater order and unity as Calcite imprints its essence into your being. You may find that during the meditation itself you don't feel any particular shift, but later on in that day you may have a flash of insight or you may realize that your awareness has increased, or that you are more at peace. Because Calcite will link spirit to matter, and each individual is at their own unique place in spiritual development, this meditation will work differently for everyone. What is sure, is that it will work.

A Window To The Past

Calcite can also be used in power vortexes and ancient sites to link parallel realities. With proper use and intention, it is possible to become aware of the realities that existed long ago before the human race entered the full materialization process. The purpose in attuning to this type of parallel reality would be to gain a greater understanding as to how to use advanced technologies, respect the life force and the elements, and create with the Divine Essence. Using Calcite as a window to the past, it is also possible to become aware of lifetimes that you may have experienced during ancient times in sacred places. Just by holding or meditating with Calcite in places such as Egypt, the Yucatan, Peru, Tibet, or power spots in the United States such as Mount Shasta or Chaco Canyon, the memory veils of time can be lifted and transcendental experiences can occur.

One of the most important factors in using Calcite as a tool to attune to the parallel reality that is simultaneously occuring in an ancient (or even a future time) is 'mental disassociation.' What this means is that all of the preconceived notions, concepts, and thought patterns that exist in the 20th century mind have to be temporarily released. The state of consciousness that exists in ancient Atlantis, Lemuria or Egypt is far different than the awareness we now have. To a large degree our perceptions are limited by the parental, social, religious and planetary programming that we have been subjected to in the 20th century. In order to plug into the true essence of consciousness as it is in another time, that pure state of 'BEING' (instead of thinking) must be achieved.

Energy vortexes existing within sacred ancient sites have recorded in the auric field all of the history that has occurred in that location. Many realities simultaneously exist in these power places. For example, if you are visiting one of the ancient healing temples in Egypt, it is easy to be in the present time, but it is also possible to tune into the Roman era, the Greek era, the early dynasties or the original Atlantian inhabitants. It is very important when working with Calcite to link into a past time, that you clearly define within your own mind exactly what specific time zone you want to tune into. What you are actually doing is attuning yourself to the reality of your choice and resonating your being at that time frequency. It is very important to clarify your intentions and visually surround yourself in a bubble of light before embarking upon time travel such as this. (See Bubble Protection, *Crystal Healing*, Vol. II, pages 38-40). Then, hold one piece of optically clear Calcite to your third eye and another to your heart and allow your being to perceive the impressions that will occur. It is necessary to have a clear open mind and be non-judgmental about what you receive. It may be like nothing you can ever remember witnessing, yet what you perceive can be in some way positively implemented into the present time.

Several benefits are gained by carrying or meditating with Calcite while traveling in power sites. First, in order to attune to another time zone it is necessary to disassociate from preexisting notions of reality. As the linear concepts of time are dissolved, it is possible to 'know' through your direct experience, that all realities simultaneously exist within the eternal moment. This, in and of itself, requires a certain degree of mastery which provides a personal challenge to expand and reach for greater truth. Secondly, experiences that allow us to tap into another time and race of beings, increases the 'know'ledge of our roots embedded in the past, or our potential in the future. Finally, many valuable lessons can be learned from places, people and situations in the past. For example, many ancient races were extremely attuned to nature and used the life force generated by the sun, water, wind and earth to create and sustain life. In our troubled world with extreme environmental pollution, such attunement to nature's laws could serve to protect and secure our natural resources.

Calcite can also be used in crystal healings to link past or future lives into the present existence. Optically clear Calcite can be placed at the third eye to integrate fragmented aspects of the self into the eternal moment of the now. With the proper therapeutics applied, the lessons of simultaneous existences in parallel realities can be applied that may not have been possible in other times. For further instructions read *Crystal Healing*, Vol. II, Part One.

Integrating The New Way

Being one of the integral members of the Mental Trinity (see *Crystal Healing*, Vol. II, pages 181-182), it has been previously written that Calcite will aid in mental transitions, adjustments and alterations and will stimulate higher brain wave frequencies when placed upon the third eye. Calcite vibrates at the highest frequency in relation to its peers in the Mental Trinity, Fluorite and Pyrite. Fluorite essentially creates mental order and maintains the connection of the intuitive with the intellect during active states. Pyrite strengthens intellectual capacity for the assimilation of higher consciousness. Calcite has the potential to ease out old attitudes and concepts that no longer serve spiritual purpose while it elevates the awareness so that a 'new way of Being' can occur.

Both Fluorite and Pyrite have a cubical matrix and share the same geometric system. If we relate to the mind and the three dimensional world as a cube (with height, width, and depth) it is easier to understand how Fluorite and Pyrite serve to strengthen and expand our three dimensional mental-physical realities. Calcite, however, has a different geometric system, which is hexagonal. In relationship to the cube, a rhomboid piece of Calcite appears as if it has stretched and extended the three dimensional reality in all possible directions. Calcite expands the cubical system to the degree that spiritual frequencies are included. Calcite boldly stands upon the threshold of dimensions and is the most effective of all the Predominant Power Stones in transmitting the energies of the three upper chakras into all of the lower energy centers.

This is obviously a time of great stress for our planet as human beings struggle to match spiritual compassion with mental technology. During the crucial years of the 1990's all old structures which do not serve the 'new way of being' will fall by the wayside. And fall they must in order to make way for a new order to unfold. Calcite will be of great service during these times as it integrates the Divine Essence with all of the new systems that will ultimately form. The marriage of science and religion, physics and metaphysics, wholistic health and traditional medicine, mind and heart, and body and soul will be the foundation upon which the new order comes into existence.

The NEW energy is here!! We no longer need to wait for it or pray for it. It is only the limited concepts of the mind and the blockages in the heart that prevent it from being acknowledged and assimilated. Calcite crystals are the most effective tools available to help link the parallel realities of an obsolete way of living in fear, with the new way of BEING in light, love and harmony with all of life. As we disassociate from the old ways of relating, the new concepts of being are there to take its place.

Use the rhomboid Calcite crystals when consciously reconstructing your reality. (See below for specific effects of different colors of Calcite). Hold them, carry them in your pocket or purse, place them on your third eye and heart, or gaze into them while meditating on their perfected parallel formations. Calcite's nature is to expand the cube, to extend the small little boxes that give our minds false security. In that expansion, more choices, opportunities and solutions are available. When you want to increase the dimension of your physical reality to include the spiritual heart, use the rhomboid Calcite crystal and it will show you how to transform your 3-D box into an entirely 'NEW WAY OF BEING!'

CALCITE'S RHOMBOID RAINBOW ARRAY

Once the light body has been activated with Selenite and the Causal Chakra receives its Kyanite Infusion, Calcite then takes over. With a complete rainbow ray of expression at its command, Calcite furthers the spiritualization process as it competently relays the message of the 'new way' into the chakra system. Calcite's essence is essential in The Crystalline Transmission as it constructs the bridge through which unlimited spiritual potential becomes an intregal part of physical reality.

Optical Clear Calcite Crystals

Optical Clear Calcite crystals are totally transparent and brilliantly radiant. These unclouded crystalline entities open and clear the space between the crown chakra and the Soul Star. When placed at the crown chakra point or held six inches above the head, they build the channels through which energy can travel from the Impersonal Divine into personalized identity. Optical Clear Calcite crystals often reflect phenomenal fluorescent rainbows. This demonstrates that pure white light can be transmitted from the Soul Star and assimilated by various color frequencies of the entire chakra system. If rainbows exist, they can be placed on any chakra center for the assimilation of light rays into the human structure.

Optical Clear Calcite crystals have positive effects in the betterment of eyesight, if the individual is ready and willing to look at the truth. They can help one 'see things clearly' and perceive reality in 'the new way. ' For that reason it is no surprise to find these crystals being used in optical devices for their special light transmitting properties. To use them in their natural form for greater and clearer perception, four small Optical Clear Calcite crystals can be used in crystal healing layouts. Place one over each eye (closed lids) and one at the third eye while holding the fourth crystal directly on the crown chakra point. Perform the necessary therapeutics and include the additional stones described in *Crystal Healing*, Volume II.

Easier to locate than Optical Clear Calcite is the regular clear variety that may have inclusions within the crystal. These Calcite crystals express clarity but are not classified in the same category as the optically clear grade. Clear Calcite can be used for the same purposes as the optical grade but will have slightly less potency and effect. Still, Clear Calcite carries its own weight in its ability to build the bridge from the Soul Star to the crown chakra and serves as a valuable meditation tool. Clear Calcite can also be placed at the third eye center when you want to receive clarification of visions, dreams, channelings or inspirational flashes.

Green Calcite

Green Calcite has already been given attention in *Crystal Healing*, Vol. II (pages 190-192). In addition to this information I would like to include the following.

It is possible to find Green Calcile in the complete rhomboid shape but most often it is found in the rough, unterminated form. Green Calcite is the most effective crystal to use in states of mental change. It works best when you are smack dab in the middle of reprogramming your mind. It helps the mind to release old fear-based concepts while in the process of consciously formulating new ideologies that include infinite possibilities. Green Calcite is there as a devoted, trustworthy friend that will provide a sense of security when you courageously say, "OK! This is what I choose to be instead!" It has a stabilizing effect in that nebulous space inbetween the stage of letting go of one reality and taking hold of a chosen new way. Being one of the mental healers, Green Calcite helps prevent an identity crisis as the charge is released and neutralized from patterns and cycles that were set into motion from past lives, genetic coding, womb experiences, and childhood.

Green Calcite's purpose is to bring in the green healing ray to ease and soothe the psyche in the letting go process. Simultaneously, it expands the cubical box of the mind into a greater sphere of knowing and understanding. Being a transition stone between what was and what is yet to become, it can be used in any crystal healing layout when a person is ready to let go, renew and rebuild preset images and mental patterns. Green Calcite is often placed at the third eye center or over the eyebrows after the use of Azurite (refer to *Crystal*

Enlightenment, Vol. I, pages 137-138) once the subconscious has been cleared.

Pink Calcite

Pink Calcite will obviously relate to the heart chakra. Calcite is formed in water and is also water soluble. Water energy relates to the emotional body. Pink Calcite can be used at the heart chakra in crystal healings or in personal meditation. This caring crystalline entity will aid in dissolving old e-motional patterns of fear, heartache, sadness and grief while simultaneously ushering in the essence of unconditional love. As it does, the heart will be healed and freed from the bondage of emotional pain and 'the new way of love' will come into being.

Pink Calcite blends the hues of Rose Quartz and Pink Tourmaline, combining the qualities of both. Rose Quartz exemplifies the inner nature of self-love and self-nurturing while Pink Tourmaline dynamically expresses that love outward into the world. Pink Calcite does both! It builds the bridge between the love we have for ourselves and the spontaneous expression of that into the world. 'The new way of loving' has its foundation in the security of honoring and loving ourselves first. With self-love as a fundamental premise, the channels of the heart will open to share that feeling with one another, the earth, all of life, and all of creation. Pink Calcite can be used at any chakra in crystal healings to integrate the power of love into the energy centers. It can also be used in meditation, carried, or worn when in the process of expanding the capacity to love. As Pink Calcite transmits its frequency into the human aura, the ability to express joy, to freely give as well as receive love, and to be nurtured by life are the natural consequences.

Peach Calcite

Peach Calcite has the same effects as Pink Calcite except it adds the brilliant golden energy of the crown chakra to be integrated into the realms of the heart. This peach hue is an exquisite new color ray that is created by blending gold and pink. Being one of the futuristic colors of the New Age, it will become more and more prevalent as we learn to blend the energies of the mind and the heart. Peach Calcite is the perfect marriage between the higher mind (gold) and the open heart (pink), creating the balanced union of conscious loving action. Peach Calcite can be used in crystal healing layouts at the crown, the heart, or at the navel to create harmony between the mind, the heart and the body. Peach Calcite becomes a valuable teacher in personal meditation as it creates the synapses that will link heart with mind, thought with feeling, and conscious perception with loving action. Peach Calcite transmits a pure new essence, one that speaks of union and hints of fantastic future existence.

Gold Calcite

Gold Calcite relates to the navel center. Also referred to as 'honey,' it is usually not terminated into the rhomboid shape but found in softly rounded hunks. Gold Calcite can be used at the navel chakra in order to integrate 'the new way' into the physical plane realities, i.e. relationships, home life, business, and life-style. As with Green Calcite, the gold assists in easing transitory phases when in the midst of change. It is a good stone to carry, wear, meditate with or sleep with while making the necessary physical plane adjustments in the process of The Crystalline Transmission. It is a stone that calms the digestive system which can be greatly affected in the assimilation of new frequencies. Honey Calcite is especially good for problems related to the gall bladder. Since the navel relates to the manifestation and expression of personal power, Honey Calcite assists in assuring that power is properly used. It is a wonderful stone to use at the navel point in crystal healing layouts to soothe turbulent changes and provide added energy for the physical assimilation of light rays. (Also refer to *Crystal Healing*, Vol. II, page 192).

Citrine Calcite

Citrine Calcite forms in perfect rhomboid shaped crystals. It links that which is perceived with the higher mind into denser frequencies of materiality. Because the golden ray of the crown is also associated with the yellow-orange of the navel, it can be used at either energy center. At the crown it will serve to stimulate the pineal gland so that expanded perspectives can be consciously perceived. Citrine Calcite transmits conscious intention into the physical cellular structure. It can be placed anywhere on the body where you want to relay new concepts or attitudes of health and well-being into the body. Therefore, Citrine Calcite crystals can be programmed with throughts and images of dis-eased tissues or organs being healthy and strong. Once programmed, place the crystal over the dis-eased part of the body and it will relay that programmed impression directly to that organ or tissue.

THE STELLAR BEAMS

Calcite is multidimensional and exceptionally versatile in nature and forms several kinds of perfect terminations. The second type of termination that I would like to give attention to is the Dogtooth Calcite, which for our purposes I have renamed "Stellar Beams. " They resemble advanced rocket ships or spacecraft that can move faster than the speed of light. These sharply terminated pieces are classified as scalenohedron and usually have some degree of transparency. The most common color the Stellar Beams reflect is the citrine gold and they are often double terminated. The other color that these projected beams will manifest is red, and these, at this time, tend to be more difficult to locate. But, as with all crystals, if you need one and are ready for it, you can bet that it will appear. With the proper attunement and intention, these powerful crystals can teach us wonders beyond our present comprehension.

A New Reality In Existence

The Stellar Beams are very different in appearance than the rhomboid shaped Calcite. And yet, the sharply terminated Stellar Beams are comprised of individual rhomboid units. If a Stellar Beam were to chip or break, you would find parallelograms, just as you do in the rhomboid Calcite crystals. These primal structures are the essential basic building blocks that create the Stellar Beams final formation. Therefore, it is through the evolution of linked parallel lines that an entirely new terminated crystal is birthed.

As previously stated, Rhomboid Calcite links the parallel realities of spirit and matter. For a moment, let's imagine what it will be like once the spiritual and the material worlds are merged. When that integration is made, we will become as living human crystals, continuously manifesting the light force in our physical lives. Then, the Crystalline Transmission will become a reality. The Stellar Beams represent that new reality, finalizing the completion of the old and renewing life in their sharply defined terminations that point to a new beginning. The Stellar Beams challenge our minds to dare to conceive of possibilities that exist outside of our limited awareness. Their essence speaks of the courage and strength that has always existed in those who have believed in their visions and lived their dreams. These highly evolved crystalline structures are a powerful statement of future potential and possibility. They have taken the primal unit of the rhomboid and shaped it into an undeniable new reality whose essence, statement, and purpose is of unified spirit and matter.

The Crystalline Transmission

The Stellar Beams can be meditated with by anyone who is willing and ready to acknowledge the new reality and integrate it; keeping only that which maintains spiritual integrity and blending it with the courageous outlook of the new way. When this process has been completed, as the sharp termination of the Stellar Beam represents, the Crystalline Essence will be fully activated and manifesting in all facets of life. The Stellar Beams are very powerful crystals to use in this type of transformative process. They will initiate greater degrees of vital force that can potentially be channeled to vibrate the material plane atomical structures at a higher rate. With the proper assimilation of this increased life energy, the spiritual vision and the physical reality can co-exist in a unified manner.

Beams Of Gold And Red

As mentioned, the most common colors that the Stellar Beams are manifesting in at this point in time are citrine and red. These are obvious colors when we correlate them to the chakra system. The citrine gold relates to the navel, of manifestation and the balance of power on the physical plane. The red corresponds to the second chakra and the creative vital force with which we manifest our power. Both of these colors have a direct effect upon the energy centers that most appropriately assimilate the new forces on the material plane.

The message that the Citrine Stellar Beams transmit is "Take the courage to change, to make the necessary shifts in consciousness and take the giant evolutionary step that is available to you, NOW!" Use the yellow ray of strength and fearlessness to boldly project this dynamic new reality into your life. Use them in your meditations to receive the vision of the new way. Carry them with you when you are in the midst of change and of letting go of the false security of old patterns. Place them to your third eye and see the hope of the future, when peace prevails and balance is restored. Use Citrine Stellar Beams at the navel, or any other appropriate location, in crystal healing layouts when a person is truly ready to make a conscious shift into living to the potential of a human-light being. Keep them around your environment so that their essence and energy can be assimilated by your being. The Stellar Beams are to be used consciously and with utmost respect. They are one of the most powerful tools available at this time to assist in moving beyond the limited preconceptions of the mind and into the infinite possibilities of spirit.

The Red Stellar Beams are usually found in cluster formations with the color resulting from a Hematite coating. With the color red activating creative energy and Hematite grounding white light forces, these crystals are exceptional tools to work with in the development of new projects on the planet that have a direct relationship to service. These are also very powerful crystals to use to initiate high degrees of vital force and creative energy that are necessary to evoke positive change upon the planet. The Red Stellar Beams usually manifest in cluster formation which symbolically relays the message of living together in harmony. Within them lies the formula for the new communities that will evolve. These crystals will be useful for centuries to come. They carry the vision and the energy for future creations that will emerge once the dream and the reality become one.

Again, these are very powerful crystalline entities and are not to be over used. Too much red energy, without the means with which to channel it into manifested creative works, can create over activation in the second chakra. This could create excess heat in the physical body resulting in possible fevers, rashes, hot flashes, etc. Start out slowly and gently in your work with these crystals. Meditate with them or place them at the second chakra for only a few minutes at a time and then put that energy directly into creative action.

Red Stellar Beams can be used at the third eye to gain the vision of what one's creative purpose is here on the earth. But, the personal responsibility to live that vision is essential in work with these crystals. Dedicated commitment is the mandatory prerequisite to work with both of these incredibly powerful and wonderful new crystals. Their crystalline transmission says to us "Do it, already!"

CALCITE LAYOUT

When a person is willing and prepared to consciously integrate the essence of 'The New Way, ' this Calcite Layout can be performed. Begin by following the initial preparatory therapeutics described in *Crystal Healing*, Vol. II, pages 15-33. Then hold an Optical Clear Calcite crystal at the crown chakra point, with a rhomboid citrine at the center of the hair line. Place green Calcite at the third eye and above each eyebrow, pink or peach at the heart center and gold at the navel. Position a Red Stellar Beam cluster at the center of the pubic bone and a double terminated Citrine Stellar Beam between the feet. Put two Black Tourmaline crystals in the hands to ensure that these energies will be properly integrated and grounded. Place any other stones that may be appropriate for each individual healing and continue to use the therapeutics discussed in Volume II. Be sure to work out a powerful maintenance plan for the recipient so that these energies can be assimilated into daily life.

There is not enough that can be said about Calcite but to save some room for other information, I will end here for now. As a Predominant Power Stone Calcite's presence is essential in the assimilation of the Soul Star energy throughout the entire chakra system. Just "BE" with Calcite and it will share with you a "New Way of Being!" In reality it is not new, it is eternal, it is only that we are now ready and able to assimilate it.

CHAPTER VII

HEMATITE

Hematite is a metamorphic mineral. When Iron is exposed to oxygen, either through the atmosphere or by contact with water, it will oxidize, giving birth to Hematite. Receiving the characteristics of both of its parents, iron and oxygen, this important iron ore rightfully inherits the strength of iron and the ethereal essence of oxygen. Transforming the nature of one of the hardest metals on the earth, Hematite is endowed through the very process of its creation with the powers of metamorphosis. Created from the earth and the gaseous ether, this Predominant Power Stone is devoted to the essence of the light body as well as to the physical body. Hematite uses the magic of metamorphosis to embody the spiritual elements in tangible form.

Being true to the earth, Hematite reflects the rays of black, grey, and brown. Staying aligned with the ethereal it can be tumbled or polished to reflect a brilliant silver sheen. It is opaque and heavier than most other stones. Hematite naturally crystallizes forming tabular or rhomboidal crystals, sometimes showing curved or striated rhomboid faces. More common however are tumbled, cabochon, or faceted stones. If you do come by a naturally terminated Hematite crystal, by all means work with it. Natural Hematite crystals are more beneficial in bridging the essence of spirit directly into the denser frequencies of the earth plane than any other crystalline form.

THE BLOOD OF THE EARTH

One way to identify minerals is the 'streak test.' Minerals with a hardness less than that of an unglazed porcelain plate (5.5) will leave a streak of fine powder when rubbed across the plate. Most of the time, the color of the powder is consistent with the color of the mineral tested. But, when grey-black Hematite is rubbed against a streak plate, a trail of blood-red is left behind it. The dust that is created when Hematite is cut or polished is also bright red. This is very significant in understanding the true nature of Hematite. What it indicates is that there is more going on with Hematite than can be perceived with the naked eye.

As previously stated, Hematite is created when Iron is oxidized as it is exposed to water. This significantly indicates that this stone is intimately related to water. Water is likened to the blood of the earth in that it nurtures all living things on the planet, just like the blood in the veins of the body feeds every living cell. The fact that the essence of this earth stone is red, instead of silver-black, indicates several things. What it signifies is that Hematite will stimulate the power of innate unseen creative energy (red) while simultaneously extending its influence into revealed manifestation (black).

Hematite

Hematite's red essence has a direct and revitalizing effect upon the human blood and circulatory system. Iron has long been known to strengthen the blood and is a necessary mineral required by humans, especially women who lose their blood every month with menstruation. Hematite can be worn, carried, made into gem remedies, used in crystal healings and meditated with for the strengthening effects of iron. It is an excellent healing stone to work with any blood ailment. Hematite will assist coagulation for bleeders, help control the loss of blood in wounds or surgical incisions, and promote the maintenance of optimum health. Not only does Hematite have a direct effect on the blood, but depending on the energy center where it is placed, it can also strengthen the will as well as the emotional, mental or spiritual bodies.

Much of the illness today is created by polluting the bloodstream whether it be a result from eating toxic foods, breathing unclean air, drinking chemicalized water or poisoning the physical system with various forms of drugs or intoxicants. Few people realize how important strong and vital blood is in the picture of wellness. If used in conjunction with good eating habits, Hematite can be an incredible partner in rebuilding the life fluid of the body. Strengthening the blood is one of the key factors in the prevention and treatment of cancer and AIDS. Rejuvenating the vital force via the circulatory system is mandatory in curing these deadly dis-eases that exist on the planet at this time. Therefore, when working with any physical dis-ease, whether it be cancer, AIDS, liver and kidney problems (the organs of blood purification), or any toxic condition, use Hematite.

Connecting the spirit into the body is Hematite's mission. As the bloodstream carries the message of spiritualized matter into the genetic coding of each cell, the physical body will be nourished and the blueprint of The Crystalline Transmission will be sown. When activating the higher octave creative forces, meditate with Hematite. When grounding the light body into the soles of your feet to direct your movement on the earth, place Hematite in your shoes to facilitate your action.

FROM SOUL STAR TO EARTH STAR

Hematite is the main stone on the planet at this time that has the power to activate the Earth Star (see page 38). In order for the light body to take up permanent residence on the physical plane it is mandatory that conscious identification be made with this chakra center. This identification will not result in attachment to worldly objects or things. Rather, it will provide a divine perspective and enable deeper understanding of the ever-changing nature of the earth's reality. The potential is great. The possibilities are unlimited when spiritual essence is fused into the roots of the physical world. Hematite has metamorphosized the very nature of hard physical reality by uniting iron and oxygen in a rare and wonderful form. It is willing to teach us how to do the same.

Hematite renders great service in the Crystalline Transmission and fulfills an essential purpose in the Predominant Power Stone Layout. Placed on the groin points, center of the thighs, knees and ankles, Hematite stones will build the bridge through which the light of the Soul Star can be connected into the roots of humanity. When three Hematite stones are placed in a triangle below the bottom of the feet and used in conjunction with Selenite, the Earth Star is activated. It is only now, upon completion of the arduous worldly cycle, that this vital earth chakra can integrate energies of the upper chakras, creating an entirely new race of beings and a unique sphere of existence.

It is advised that individualized meditation and attunement with Hematite precede the Predominant Power Stone

Hematite

Layout to begin the process of purifying and strengthening the blood for this transfusion of light. Hematite has the power to channel spiritual energy directly into the blood to stimulate all of the cells of the body with a vitalized force. As this occurs there will be a profound yet subtle shift in the genetic coding that has been inherited from the ages of forgetfulness. With each primal unit of life within the physical form nourished with the very substance of light, accelerated changes will begin to occur. Then new patterns will be infiltrated, replacing old encoded programs that have dominated our consciousness for millenniums.

As this process occurs and the reality of 'The New Way' is initiated, Hematite continues to be a solid companion as a new body chemistry is created. Carrying, wearing, meditating or sleeping with Hematite in the days, weeks and months that follow this advanced layout will prove to be extremely helpful. It seems that one of the hardest parts of having spiritual experiences is that they pass and we are left only with the memory and the anxious anticipation of the next revelation. Dedicated time with Hematite will prove to be most beneficial as the changes are made real in the moment to moment reality of daily existence.

Used in regular crystal healing layouts three Hematite stones can be placed below the feet in a triangular shape to channel energy into the Earth Star. It is beneficial when using Hematite in this manner to have the recipient inhale the breath from the Soul Star down through the center line to the base of the spine (see *Crystal Healing*, Vol. II, pages 24-27). But, instead of exhaling back up the spine, allow the breath to be released down the legs and out the soles of the feet to connect with the Earth Star six inches below the body. Of course this type of breathing technique would also be good for anyone who needed to associate more with the physical body and/or get grounded.

BUILDING A REFLECTOR SHIELD

As inner transformation occurs it is necessary to continuously reidentify with that which is being birthed instead of that which is falling away. Many changes will be occurring on the planet in the next decade. Established systems and ways of life will alter, shift or cease to exist as all of the earthly structures are tested with the true integrity of spirit. This is indeed the labor pain that the earth is experiencing as she gives birth to a new breed and a new world. And yet, it is so easy to become attached to people, things, events and patterns of being that have provided us with false security. Hematite, with its strength and metamorphic powers can be used in these times to strengthen and fortify the vision and the hope of that which is being birthed within us as well as on the planet.

It is possible to build a reflector shield using Hematite. This shield will help one to stay focussed during times of change and serve as a protection against psychic negativity or lower frequency environments. A Hematite reflector shield also helps to establish defined personal boundaries so that you do not take on another person's feelings or energy. Building this shield does not mean that you won't feel, be aware of, or interact with what is going on around you. Instead, it means that you will be able to better maintain your own identity, energy and conscious connection to your source as you live in the world in these transition times. Hematite assists in creating a will of iron so that conscious choices can be made that will enable personal goals to be achieved.

Hematite is an incredibly shiny and reflective stone that was actually used to make mirrors in ancient times. This reflective attribute is what enables Hematite to cast back negative impressions that have external origins while simultaneously providing inner strength. Using Hematite in this way will help you to see what is yours and what is not, where you need to personally grow and make changes and what is being imposed from other's expectations and demands.

To build a reflective shield, have the receiver lie down and place Hematite stones on each one of the chakra centers. Place Hematite stones in each hand, touching the heel of each foot and another six inches below the feet to activate the Earth Star. A natural Pyrite cube or cluster is positioned at the crown chakra and touches the top of the head. Put twelve more Hematite stones in the auric space around the body, at least six inches away from any body part. Two should be in alignment with the eyes, two with the shoulders, two out from the solar plexus, two even with the hips, two parallel with the knees and the final two six inches from the ankles. The breath is long and deep, focusing the inhale by drawing energy from the crown and taking it all the way down into the soles of the feet. On the exhale radiate that energy out from every pore of the body to connect with the Hematite stones placed in the auric field. Breathe in this fashion for eleven minutes. Each breath will draw strength and power first into the body and then out into the aura for continued reinforcement.

Practicing this layout every day will be beneficial for those who are constantly met with the challenge of staying true to the self while living in the outside world. It is of added benefit to carry or wear a Hematite stone as a constant reminder that the Hematite forcefield is activated. Then at any time needed, whether entering a darkened subway terminal or engaging in a confrontative discussion, mentally visualize the shield and it will serve its protective function. It is also possible to tape a piece of Hematite to the solar plexus or heart center when anticipating interaction with intense people or situations. The Hematite reflective shield projects the spiritual force into the aura at maximum capacity enabling one to stay more centered and loving while actively interacting with life. In so doing, it becomes increasingly easier to discern what honestly needs to be dealt with, and what outside influences can be disregarded.

STILL MORE . . .

As with all of the Predominant Power Stones, Hematite serves many functions. It is also a very powerful third eye stone. When placed at the brow it will serve different purposes, depending on who is working with it and what they need. For some, it will establish contact and facilitate communication with extraterrestrials. For others it will act as a mirror to the subconscious mind in order to perceive the self more clearly. And still for some, it will strengthen the power of positive thought projection.

Because of Hematite's ability to keep all of the subtle bodies connected to the physical body it takes first place as the jet-lag stone. Wear or carry Hematite in your pockets or tape stones to the soles of your feet before embarking on air travel. It is also beneficial to take a bath with at least three Hematite stones in a tub full of warm water as soon as possible after flying long distances. Hematite's ability to keep the bodies intact also proves useful before and after surgery and anesthesia, when suffering from shock or extremely stressful conditions, after near death experiences, or for mothers and babies after cesarean births. In addition, it is very useful for people who space out, get dizzy, have low blood pressure or get easily disassociated from the physical world.

Last, but not least, Hematite makes a wonderful sleeping partner when combating insomnia. In this case it helps to ease the strain created from an overactive mind while it redirects its grounding force into the body so that it can rest. It is an ideal stone to place under the pillow if encountering demons of fear on the astral plane while asleep (or while awake). Hematite is like a shield of armor that will defend and protect so that strength can be drawn from inner resources. Placed under the pillows of children who do not sleep through the night or who are plagued by nightmares,

Hematite

Hematite grounds and stabilizes energy currents running through the body and thus will facilitate peaceful sleep.

CHAPTER VIII

THE ADVANCED PREDOMINANT POWER STONE INITIATION

The whole idea of the Crystalline Transmission is to bring the light of spirit into the physical body to elevate and transform the very nature of life on the earth. This Predominant Power Stone Layout is the means through which that can occur. By activating the light body at the Soul Star with Selenite and channeling that essence into the Causal Chakra with the help of Kyanite, the mental blueprint can be recreated in harmony with the laws of spirit. The multidimensional nature of Calcite integrates that light throughout the entire chakra system to be grounded into the roots of the earth with Hematite.

More than just a crystal layout, this is a powerful initiation that will simultaneously activate the three upper chakras, channel that spiritual energy through the physical body, and ground it at the Earth Star. Those who will perform this initiation for others, as well as those who receive it, must be educated, prepared, and committed to the process of The

Crystalline Transmission. It has required years of personal research and lifetimes of practice with crystals to recall this advanced technology. As with all of my work thus far, I now offer this information to you with a prayer and with conviction that this knowledge will only be used in accordance with Divine Will and for betterment of all beings concerned.

PREPARATION

This initiation is not for people who are in the phase of healing where they are letting go, clearing, releasing and reprogramming. It is however highly recommended that several crystal healing sessions precede this advanced layout to assist the recipient in the mental, emotional and physical cleansing that would naturally come before an initiation of this kind. It is also necessary that both the performer and the recipient be familiarized with the power of crystals and stones and have personal practice in assimilating higher frequency crystalline energy. This initiation layout should be performed only on those who feel clear, guided, and 'know' within their hearts that they are ready, open and prepared to undergo an extremely powerful influx of energy. These individuals must make a conscious commitment to their identity as human light-beings on the earth plane and be willing to ground their Soul Star energy into the roots of Terra. Under no circumstances should this layout (or variations of it) be used to beam out of the body in an attempt to disconnect with the earth reality, which is the obvious arena for evolutionary growth at this time.

Listed below are several ways to prepare for The Predominant Power Stone Initiation:

1. Become very familiar, through your own experience, with all four of the Predominant Power Stones. Work with the

stones individually, meditate with them, use them in appropriate situations, and align yourself with their frequencies.

2. Practice the Circulating Breath Exercises (see pages 47-48) as you simultaneously attune to the Soul Star and the Earth Star. If possible, get into a habit of performing the Sunrise and Sunset Meditations (see pages 46-48). Be sure that as you attune to the Great Central Sun in the meditations that your feet are firmly planted on the ground and your Earth Star is shining. It is ideal to practice the breath exercises with the Sun Meditations for at least ten days prior to performing this advanced layout. If it is not possible to do the Sun Meditations, practice the breath exercises for at least eleven minutes upon waking, and before retiring.

3. Prepare and strengthen your physical body by eating healthy foods, drinking eight glasses of pure water per day, and exercising regularly. You may find it helpful to do a three day juice fast before this initiation. However, it is important that you break the fast at least two days before the layout is performed so that the body is restrengthened and fortified. With the exception of medically prescribed medication, no drugs should be used for at least 40 days prior to this initiation.

4. If possible, work with a Certified Crystal Healer in the performance of this layout. If not possible, find someone that you intuitively trust, who knows the crystals and stones well, is familiar with the information in The Crystal Trilogy, and who understands and accepts the responsibility for the magnitude of the endeavor to be undertaken. It is necessary that this person also be willing to take the time to personally attune to the Predominant Power Stones and feel comfortable in the position of facilitator.

5. Of course your personal guidance is the most important factor. You will know when you are ready for this initiation. You may need months or years of preparation or you may now be ready and only need to know the specifics of the

layout in order to proceed. Whatever the case may be, your being will undoubtedly let you know if this initiation is for you. It may not be, and that too is perfect for you. It may be that you will utilize the Predominant Power Stones in many other dynamic and effective ways.

6. A prior commitment must be made to incorporate a strong maintenance plan into the daily life-style for at least forty days following the Predominant Power Stone Initiation. Whatever the conscious effects are, there are subtle and deep shifts that will occur within whoever experiences this Crystalline Transmission. It is mandatory that the way be made clear, through personalized disciplinary action, for the higher frequencies to find routes for manifestation. The Circulating Breath Exercises and the Sun Meditations can be applied in the maintenance plan as well as whatever else personally applies.

The results of this layout may be subtle and profound or dramatic and overt depending upon each individual's state of personal advancement. The effects may be most obvious as currents of energy are firmly established between the Soul Star and the Earth Star. Or, the Kyanite Infusion at Causal Chakra may alter mental patterns as the nature of your thoughts take on a new dimension. It is also possible that complete empowerment occurs, but it is more likely that the effects will be cumulative as the maintenance plan is incorporated into the daily life-style. If you feel guided to reenact this initiation, wait at least forty days to fully integrate the effects of your first experience before repeating the layout.

I wish all of you who experience this Predominant Power Stone Initiation the very best. Know that my prayers are with you and my heart feels excitement and joy when thinking about the possibility of the Crystalline Transmission becoming a reality in your life!

THE LAYOUT

Following is a list of all of the stones that you will need to accurately perform this layout.

Two Selenite wands; a large one (at least six inches long and one inch wide) to be placed nine inches above the top of the head with the termination pointing towards the center back of the head. The second one can be smaller, and is to be held in the hand of the facilitator for work in the aura of the recipient.

One Kyanite wand which is to be placed below the Selenite and above the top of the head, with one end touching the Causal Chakra.

One optically clear rhomboid Calcite is to be placed at the crown chakra or at the top of the forehead at the hair line.

Three green rhomboid Calcite crystals are to be placed at the third eye point and over the center top of each eyebrow, forming a triangle.

Three clear rhomboid Calcite crystals are used. One is placed at the throat chakra and the other two are held in the palm of each hand.

Three pink/peach rhomboid Calcite crystals; one will be placed at the heart chakra point with the other two above and to either side of the first, forming a triangle.

One double terminated citrine Stellar Beam will reside at the solar plexus with one point directed towards the heart and the other toward the navel.

Three honey Calcite crystals (preferably rhomboids); one directly over the navel and the other two below and to either side of that point, forming a triangle.

One red Stellar Beam (either a single terminated, double terminated or a cluster will serve the purpose) is to be placed on the second chakra point.

Twelve pieces of Hematite are needed (tumbled stones may be used). Place one in the center of the pubic bone with one on each groin point, forming a triangle. Place one on the center of each thigh, one below each knee, one at each ankle and one at the heel of each foot with the final one six inches below the feet, forming a triangle with the heels.

If you choose, and if it is appropriate, naturally double terminated clear quartz crystals may be placed in-between each of the chakra points to facilitate increased circulation of energy.

THERAPEUTICS

The environment should be prepared in such a manner as to be conducive to meditation. It is important during this Initiation that there be no interruptions. It is therefore advisable to put a 'please do not disturb' sign on the door and if need be, unplug the telephone. It is also ideal for both the recipient of the Predominant Power Stone Layout and the facilitator to sit together beforehand and call upon protection and guidance (see *Crystal Healing*, Vol. II, page 30). Once rapport has been created and both parties feel relaxed, the recipient should lay down and begin long, slow, deep, complete abdominal breathing.

Once the breathing becomes stabilized, the recipient should begin to simultaneously focus on the Soul Star and the Earth Star while the facilitator places the stones in the proper formation. After the stones have been placed the recipient will take a long, full, deep breath and hold it for fifteen seconds while concentrating on bringing energy from the Soul Star into the Causal Chakra. The breath is held as light is channeled through the Selenite and into the Kyanite wand to be consolidated at the center back of the head. On the exhale, the light is directed back up to the Soul Star. The recipient will continue to breathe and visualize in this fashion for three minutes while establishing a connection between the Soul Star and the Causal Chakra.

During this time the facilitator will hold the second Selenite wand in his/her right hand. When the recipient inhales, the facilitator will trace a line of energy from above the Soul Star, and over the top of the Selenite and Kyanite wands. During the time that the breath is retained, the facilitator will hold the Selenite wand directly on the Causal Chakra point. As the recipient exhales, the facilitator will move the Selenite wand back up to the Soul Star position and repeat the process on the following breath.

To complete this three minute Causal Chakra empowerment, the recipient will inhale deeply and hold the breath for fifteen seconds. On the exhale, he/she will visualize the energy traveling down the center front of the body and through the legs to connect with the Earth Star below the feet. On the following inhale, the Earth Star energy is brought up the back of the legs, through the spine and the head to reconnect with the Soul Star. Continue to circulate the energy of the Soul Star down the front of the body until it reaches the Earth Star on each exhale. On each inhale, bring the earth energy up the back of the legs, into the spine, and through the head to connect once again at the Soul Star. Breathe in this fashion for eleven to twenty one minutes with the mind completely focussed on the energy circulating with the breath and the marriage of the polar stars.

The amount of time spent doing this is totally dependent upon each individual and their ability to channel and integrate the energies. If the mind becomes clouded with thoughts, or if emotions surface making it difficult to concentrate on the breath, gracefully remove the Predominant Power Stones and conclude initiation for the time being. It may mean that it is necessary to undergo more crystal healing sessions or to take more time with the preparatory stages.

During the time that the recipient is concentrating on circulating the breath, the facilitator will again be using the Selenite wand held in the right hand. In correlation with the recipient's breath, the wand is moved six inches above the recipient's body, from the Soul Star to the Earth Star and back again. In other words, while the recipient is inhaling, the facilitator will trace lines of energy up the legs, above the center line and over the face, to connect with the Soul Star point above the top of the head. As the recipient is exhaling, the facilitator will run the Selenite wand through the aura back down over the head, the center line, the legs and feet, and will touch the bottom Hematite stone at the Earth Star point. This motion should be continued until clear lines of energy have been established between the Soul Star and the Earth Star (usually about five to ten minutes). Then, with the final tracing, the Selenite wand is placed in the triangle of Hematite stones formed between the heels and the Earth Star point, with the termination touching the lower Hematite stone.

The facilitator should then observe the breath of the recipient and make sure that it remains steady, full and complete. Under no circumstances should the breath become shallow or light. If this occurs, remind the recipient to breathe deeply and completely. If necessary, establish verbal communication and inquire as to what is happening within the recipient. If there is no response, or if it is uncomfortable for full focussed breathing to be restored, remove the stones, massage the recipient's feet and have him/her gradually open both eyes. In most cases however, the facilitator will be the time keeper and not allow the recipient to exceed the twenty one minute time limit.

CLOSURE

The recipient of this initiation will intuitively know when maximum results have been achieved. If that time occurs before twenty one minutes, the recipient will communicate to the facilitator to begin closure. When finalizing the circulating breath exercise, the recipient will simultaneously focus on both the Soul Star and the Earth Star for at least one minute while allowing the breath to be full and deep. As these polar stars align and harmonize, resume normal, relaxed, unconcentrated breathing.

The facilitator will remove the stones and ask the recipient to slowly open the eyes. Then the facilitator will gently squeeze the arms and legs, and massage the recipient's feet. Following this, the facilitator will place one hand on top of the head and the other on the pubic bone and hold for three minutes. Have the recipient then slowly sit up and briskly rub his/her spine, from top to bottom. Give the recipient a drink of water or herbal tea and mutually discuss the experience. Work out an appropriate maintenance plan to be incorporated into a 40-day follow up program.

The recipient should plan ample time following this initiation to go for a walk and be outside in nature. It is important to eat protein afterward; tofu, grains or nuts would be best. It is also best if the rest of the day (or night) could be taken for quiet assimilation time.

For the days and weeks following the Predominant Power Stone Layout, be aware of the subtle to overt changes that will occur. Take time to integrate these changes. The more meditative personal quiet time taken, the better. It is also very appropriate during this time to keep a journal of the changes in mind, heart and body.

The most important thing to be aware of in the execution of this advanced procedure is that you are striving to create the necessary circumstances in your life to come into a state of peace and completion within your own being. First, focussed attention on the self is required. Then, as more and more individuals come into a joyful harmonious relationship with creation, a mass consciousness will come into existence that will transmit a new frequency out into the world that can't help but create positive global changes.

We are all in the process of personal initiation. It may or may not take the form of this Predominant Power Stone Layout. That is not what is important. What is crucial at this time, is that the light body be invited to reside permanently within the physical body. At this point in time, dedicated commitment to this process is required. It is necessary that each person, in whatever way is appropriate, prioritize personal wholeness and then take physical action to recreate life in a way that manifests peace, love and joy. It is not enough anymore to merely sit, pray, visualize, and affirm, as important as that is. Positive intentions must be converted into externalized actions. Then, all of the things that you KNOW within the depths of your being to be possible will be within your power to manifest. It is possible to mend the hole in the ozone, to feed the hungry, to end the threat of nuclear war and heal the environment. If you can think it, feel it, envision it, and most importantly know it and be it, all things become possible.

SECTION III
THE MASTER CRYSTALS

INTRODUCTION TO
THE MASTER CRYSTALS

The first six Master Crystals were featured in *Crystal Healing*, Vol. II. Since the completion of that book I have discovered, researched and written about six more, making a total of twelve Master Crystals. All of these are quartz crystals and connect white light to the physical plane. Each one of the Master Crystals will demonstrate specific principles, relay powerful concepts and transmit the essence of a divine truth. Several of the Master Crystals have specific geometric contructs forming the angles on the faces of the termination which can be interpreted symbolically as well as numerologically. Some are less defined in their characteristics. The similarity between them all is that they are all "masters" in their own right and are here as teachers to our evolving consciousness. The knowledge on how to recognize and use them indicates that we are ready to learn the teachings that they have to offer humanity.

The Crystalline Transmission

I am pleased to present the final six Master Crystals. Their uses as well as their messages are varied and yet they all point us in the same direction, directly into the heart of truth. The Dow Crystal transmits the pure essence of Christ Consciousness. The Tantric Twins teach us how to harmonize with our own higher selves as well as with others. The Isis Crystal relays the secrets of self-healing and the mysteries of womanhood. The Cathedral Lightbraries are open data banks through which divine knowledge can be programmed and relayed into our consciousness. The Devic Temples are the vehicles through which discarnate devas can indirectly guide us on the spiritual path. And last but not least, the Time Links assist us in dissolving the illusion of linear time so that the contributions that our alter-identities have to offer can be bestowed upon the present lifetime. Use these crystals with the utmost respect and awareness. They are here as a gift and a blessing to those who will be guided to learn their sacred teachings.

CHAPTER IX
THE DOW CRYSTAL

The Dow Crystal was briefly mentioned in *Crystal Healing*, Vol. II, page 118. This specialized crystal manifests perfect geometry with the six facets comprising the termination alternating between triangles and seven-sided faces. The Dow Crystal is a combination of the Channeling Crystal and the Transmitter Crystal (see *Crystal Healing*, Vol. II, pages 101-119). The triangle marking the back face of the Channeling Crystal is the same triangle in the center of the Transmitter Crystal. Incorporating both channeling and transmitting properties, the Dow Crystal can be used to express the deepest inner truth, as well as being capable of receiving, containing, and projecting programmed information. When the initial work was done with the Dow Crystals they were rare and hard to find. Now, these Master Crystals seem to be in greater abundance, and well they should be, since they serve a great purpose in The Crystalline Transmission.

Before I present any further new information on the Dow Crystals, I would like to acknowledge and thank my long time friend, Jane Ann Dow, for her continued support and assistance in gathering the information on these geometrically perfect crystals. Jane Ann's attunement to the Dow Crystals (named in her honor) was essential in bringing to you the full spectrum of wisdom concerning their purpose and use.

NUMEROLOGICAL AND GEOMETRIC MEANING

The Dow Crystals serve an even greater purpose than the combined effects of channeling and transmitting, which can be discovered when more attention is given to the numerological and geometric significance. The faces comprising the termination of a Dow crystal are all seven-sided or triangular. The number seven is symbolic of the ultimate inner truth that is attained when the seeker looks within the inner sanctums of the self. The three represents the trinity and the expression and manifestation of that inner truth. When adding the three seven-sided faces with the three triangles, the sum of thirty is reached (7X3 plus 3X3). Thirty is a three with a circle after it, which in numerology can be further reduced to one single three. Thirty signifies the trinity in the constant motion of a circle. The circle contains within it everything that comes into being in the cycle of creation; the totality of expression, from alpha to omega, from life into death and rebirth. The sum thirty pertains directly to the wheel of life in all of its varied aspects. What this means in relationship to working with the Dow Crystal is that all facets of one's being and life can be positively affected. By reducing the number thirty to a three, all relationships pertaining to 'a trinity' are influenced by the Dow. This could relate to body, heart and mind, or

THE DOW CRYSTAL

conscious, subconscious and superconscious, or to the lower chakras, upper chakras and transpersonal chakras.

Of all of the quartz crystals, the Dow manifests the most perfect geometry. The symmetrical patterning of the Dow Crystal is unique among all crystalline forms. It has translated the reality of spiritual perfection into material form in the angles comprising the faces. Recognizing the perfection in the mineral kingdom through the Dow, helps us to entertain the possibility that we can also physically manifest that state of integrity, unity, balance and order. The Dow also makes another statement. It transmits the message that before we can manifest that divinity (the triangles) we must first access our own inner truth (the septagons). However, there is a basic limited concept ingrained into our beings that first must be reprogrammed. This age old program dates back to the time when the Roman Catholic Church first canonized the Bible. Extracting from the original documents regarding the life of Jesus the Christ, only fragmented information survived; that which best suited the ambitions of the church. Excluded from the teachings was such valuable information as that on reincarnation and the fact that we are all candidates for Christhood.

REDEFINING CHRIST CONSCIOUSNESS

There is no doubt that Jesus the Christ was a perfected being (as well as several other masters and saints that have lived upon the earth). The life of Jesus Christ exemplified unconditional love. There is no question in my mind that all twelve of his chakras were activated and working in impeccable order. How else could he manifest the miracles and the healing that he did? He lived the reality of The Crystalline Transmission and attempted to teach others how to do so as well. We can further relate if we look at one of Jesus's most famous statements. "I and My Father are One, " he said. It is obvious that he was one with his source, which in this context is defined as 'father. ' Through the activation of the three transpersonal chakras, each one of us can also become one with that same source. With the simultaneous activation of the Earth Chakra, fully ordained Christhood is achieved and the manifestation of miracles and healing can occur on a mass level.

The Christ Consciousness is very much associated with the light body and the Soul Star. It is at this chakra where the universal, omnipresent, omnipotent essence of the Stellar Gateway becomes individualized in the lighted 'Christ Self. ' The Soul Star translates that cosmic energy into the Christ Consciousness to be relayed directly into the heart of humanity. Just as Jesus the Christed was the messenger on this planet for that state of being, so can we be. Jesus lived at the beginning of the Age of Pisces and served as a singular example of the reality of The Crystalline Transmission. Now, two thousand years later, as we enter into the Golden Age of Aquarius, that crystalline reality becomes possible for the masses. This is the true meaning of 'the second coming of the Christ. ' It is in the inner sanctums of our hearts that the Christ Consciousness, actualized at the Soul Star, finds full expression in the miraculous power of love. As the Christ Consciousness is resurrected within us, the rebirth of total spiritual awareness will take place at the third eye and God's perfect plan will be revealed. As the light body is integrated into the physical body, the living Christ will manifest in glorious creations in our lives.

The Dow Crystal, existing in its state of perfection, is a most valuable tool to work with in the actualization of Christ Consciousness upon this earth. We are already familiar with Selenite which activates the light body at the Soul Star Chakra. However, Selenite is very limited to only that initial activation process and works primarily in the realm of light. The perfect geometrical patterning of the Dow Crystal matches the high vibrational frequency of the pure Christed state of consciousness. But, the Dow is a quartz crystal and is fully related to the earth and her elements. In being composed of earth's own silicon dioxide as well as pure white light, it has the unique ability to translate the essence of that transcended state of Christ Consciousness into the trinity of mind, heart, and body. Because of the inherent circular energy existing in the Dow (the 3Q) this crystal can match the spiralling rotational energy of each chakra vortex and transmit the Christ Consciousness into all of the energy centers. The Dow Crystal, being an earth light that vibrates at the Christ frequency, also greatly assists in the integration and assimilation of that energy onto the earth.

The manifestation of Christ Consciousness is the ultimate expression of heaven on earth, the final phase of The Crystalline Transmission. As the restricting traditional Christian dogmas are revised and reprogrammed to include all of humanity, the reality of Christ Consciousness can unfold in our lives and on our earth. There is not just one son of God. We are all sons and daughters of our source father. We are all capable of living in accordance with the spiritual laws of unconditional love just as our soul brother Jesus did. The Dow Crystals are here to assist us in living in perfection by transmitting the essence of spirit into the reality of the earth and that which can be seen, touched, felt, and understood.

WORKING WITH DOW CRYSTALS

Even though you find a Dow Crystal with the faces alternating from septagons to triangles, some Dows will be predominately Channeling Crystals with one of the seven-sided faces being extra large. Some of them will have prevailing Transmitter Crystal properties, with a larger triangle sided by two large septagons, while the rest of the faces are smaller. When practicing the following exercises and meditations it is most effective to use Dow Crystals that have even sided symmetrical faces. In other words, it would be best to use crystals where all of the seven-sided faces are of equal size and all of the triangles are in the same proportion.

The Dow Crystal is an excellent meditation companion which can be held in the left hand during internalized quiet time to transmit into the consciousness Christ-like impressions. If one is lying down, the Dow can be placed above the top the the head in the Soul Star area, with the termination pointing towards the body, to integrate the Christ light into the consciousness. Because the Dow maintains the pattern of perfection through its flawless geometry, it is extremely useful to use this master crystal when in the process of consciously reprogramming our minds. It can be used in conjunction with Kyanite at the Causal Chakra to assure that the newly formed thoughts and concepts maintain the integrity of Christ-like purity. The Dow Crystal can also be placed at any of the chakra centers, from the crown down to the base, to transmit that standard of excellence into the individual characteristics of each energy center.

Holding the immaculate perfection of the pattern of light, the Dow Crystal can be a tremendous aid in healing the heart chakra. So much of the pain stored at the heart and solar plexus can be transmuted if we can have but one experience of divine love. When we do, a deep inner knowing is seeded in the heart out of which blossoms acceptance and understanding of the divine plan. Experiencing the Divine Essence in our hearts, even for a brief moment, lays the foundation upon which unconditional love can be built. The Dow Crystal is like a mirror that reflects perfection. It can be used in crystal healings at the heart and solar plexus areas to give the feeling nature of the heart chakra a new pattern to model itself after.

Often times, so much of the pain that we feel originates outside of ourselves as we overly identify with the sufferings of others and the woes of the world. The Dow Crystal is a powerful companion to use while consciously divorcing ourselves from the pain of others. This does not mean that we will lose concern, but rather that the external pain of others will not be claimed as our own. This is a necessary step in the process of The Crystalline Transmission. If we truly recognize our perfection and live in accordance with the laws of love, there will be no room for fear, anger, and pain. It is true that pain is a great teacher, but at some point the lessons are learned and it is time to graduate to a higher level of realization. Ultimately pain teaches us that we can, in fact, live without it. Through dedicated work with the Dow Crystal, understanding evolves that enables us to know that essentially everything exists in a state of perfection. This knowing changes the reality of pain and a shift in awareness occurs that alters our relationship to suffering. The Dow Crystal assists us in identifying with and becoming the perfection instead of living with the pain.

Malachite is a powerful stone to work with in conjunction with the Dow Crystal during this process. (see Malachite, *Crystal Enlightenment*, Vol. I, pages 142-146). Malachite is a stone that has the capacity to surface suppressed feelings from the solar plexus area. In that way it is a stone of movement. In order to change and come into alignment with that which is eternally true, there has to be movement. When separating your pain from others, Malachite will stir the pot, so to speak, so that you can discern what is yours and what is not. When used together in crystal healings, the random motion of e-motions catalyzed by Malachite, is brought into perfect order by the Dow. Four small Dow generators can surround a Malachite stone at the solar plexus, or once the e-motions surface, Malachite can be removed and replaced with the Dow Crystal. After the crystal healing, the recipient can stand up while the healer moves the Dow Crystal through the aura, from the Soul Star to the bottom of the feet. In this way the energy field is imprinted with the pattern of perfection. This is an exercise that need not be limited to crystal healings. It can be practiced with another person whenever the need arises to create a greater sense of harmony and order.

THE CRYSTAL PYRAMID MEDITATION

When holding the Dow Crystal down at an angle and looking through one of the seven-sided faces at the triangle in the back of the crystal, a phenomenon occurs. What can be witnessed is a three dimensional pyramid of light existing inside of the crystal.

The pyramids in ancient civilizations were perfected geometrical structures that were built on this planet by advanced races to usher cosmic energy onto the earth (see Earth Star, pages 38-42). When looking at a pyramid, architectural perfection can be witnessed. We can observe the four corners rooted into the earth as well as the apex reaching into the heavens. The pyramid of light that lives inside of Dow Crystals once again relays to our consciousness the perfect patterning of not only light, but of the possibility for that to manifest in three dimensional form.

Human beings are tactile creatures. We learn from our experiences and through our sensory feelings. How can we learn to exist in form and maintain that perfected patterning of light while doing so? By experiencing what it feels like. The Crystal Pyramid Meditation is designed to give us the experience of what it feels like to be that perfection of unified light and form through which balance, harmony and order can be embodied. Once experienced, we then have a reference point and can more easily re-create that reality. If we feel it long enough, soon we will be capable of identifying with it and before long, it will become an automatic response and way of being.

In this meditation your consciousness will actually enter into the pyramid of light inside of the Dow Crystal. Sit in an easy cross-legged position with the spine straight. Imagine yourself to be a pyramid with the top of your head being the apex and the crossed legs and the buttocks being the base. Set this image and maintain it during the length of the meditation. Holding the Dow at a downward angle in your left hand, gaze through one of the seven-sided faces at the opposing triangle. (Note: the bigger the back triangle is, the larger the pyramid will be). As you focus your full concentration, allow your awareness to pass through the body of the Dow and penetrate into the pyramid of light. Once inside, maintain a still silent presence. Just be open and let the essence of the Dow be impressed upon your aura. Do not try to define the experience with your mind or to control it with your feelings. Just 'be' inside the lighted pyramid and allow that perfected patterning to create its own form. Feel what it is like to be in a state of perfection and allow that reality to be transmitted into every facet of your being.

To close this meditation, bring your awareness back into your body and take several long deep breaths. Gently close your eyes and feel yourself to be that pyramid of light that you have just experienced. Superimpose the image of the pyramid of light over your meditating body while you simultaneously connect with your apex at the crown and the roots of the base chakra on the earth. Have a Smoky Quartz or a Black Tourmaline handy and replace the Dow Crystal in your hand with one of the dark stones to assist in grounding the energies.

The Dow Crystal

The Crystalline Transmission is facilitated by the practice of The Crystal Pyramid Meditation. As the perfect patterning of light is integrated into our beings through work with the Dow Crystal, that Christ-like energy begins to be transmitted through us. Then, when other people come into contact with our own personal 'Dows' (our perfected patterning) they will in some positive way be influenced, whether it be subliminal and subconscious or profoundly direct and evident.

CHAPTER X
THE TANTRIC TWINS

The nature of relationships is drastically changing in this day and age. What has been adhered to as 'the traditional way' is no longer accepted by the masses. The increased rate of divorce, single parenting, gay relationships, open relationships, and various other forms of coupling, indicates that what was the customary model in the Piscean Age is altering to meet the needs of a new tomorrow. We are in the midst of this transition and it is as if the energies of Shiva, Kali, or Pan have stepped in to stir everything up and create the chaos out of which a new order of relationship can emerge.

In the midst of this change comes to us another Master Crystal which has the keys to unlock the secrets of 'right relationship' and true union with another. The Tantric Twins, by the very quality of their design and nature, relay the wisdom so vitally needed at this time to teach us 'the new way' of creating both the personal relationship that we have with ourselves and that which we share with others. As the crystalline energies of the Tantric Twins are assimilated into our auras, we will be capable of creating a new form of bonding that is in accordance with the divine order of The Golden Age of Aquarius.

TACTILE TRAITS OF THE TANTRIC TWINS

In *Crystal Enlightenment*, Vol. I, we became familiar with the single generator, which has only one termination, and the cluster in which many single terminated crystals share a common base. The Single Generators symbolize individuality and the Clusters exemplify the evolved community. The Tantric Twin Crystals are unique unto themselves. They relate to personal relationships and to the harmonious union of two separate, yet intimately bonded individuals. The Tantric Twins share a common base and yet have two distinct terminations at the apex. Both terminations may or may not be the same height, the important factor is that there is a pairing of single points.

Another strikingly beautiful characteristic often (but not always) displays itself in the Tantric Twins. Where the single crystals meet, there will, on occasion, be brilliant fluorescent rainbows. What could be a better sign of harmonious union than the prismatic interplay of light and color manifesting in an iridescent rainbow? These crystals, more than those without rainbows, will transmit a sense of joy while relaying the many rays and ways that relationships can be colored.

TRANSLATING TRUE TANTRA

Tantra means union, or the harmonious mergence of energies. In working with the Tantric Twins this can mean several

THE TANTRIC TWIN CRYSTAL

things. First, the most important relationship is the one that we have with ourselves. How we feel about, and relate with our own inner beings will be reflected into every other relationship that we encounter; especially those with the opposite sex. Males and females are polarity energies, mirroring back and forth to one another personal insecurities and inadequacies. If we are in a state of personal balance within ourselves it is then possible to find unity with another person. If not, we will constantly externalize our own state of being onto someone else.

Two individual terminations bond together in the Tantric Twin Crystal. This symbolizes an important teaching. If indeed the Tantric Twins contain the mysteries of divine connectedness with another, it becomes apparent that each individual must first be aligned with their own source. These twin crystals impress upon us the necessity for each single termination to reach its own apex of completion. Just so, in seeking true partnership with another, it is vital that personal attunement to our own inner essence be first established.

The greatest tantric union is when the soul becomes one with the infinite spirit. The first job of the Tantric Twins is to assist each individual in establishing that primal state of unity. In this sense, the dual terminations represent the soul fused with Divine Essence. To the degree that this primary relationship is intact, determines how we relate externally to all others. Once we gain true tantra with our source, we cannot help but know that everyone else, regardless of seeming differences, also shares that common source in Divine Essence. Any Tantric Twin Crystal will transmit the energies necessary to assist individuals in forming primal integrity in the vital relationship between soul and source.

The second stage of tantric union is in the realm of interpersonal relationships. Once personal union with the source is achieved, it is then possible to attract another being who is also attuned to his/her own essence. Like attracts like and these types of relationships can be defined as soul-partners. Whether the relationship is heterosexual, homosexual, or non-sexual, common likeness will seek itself out. When two souls are first in harmony with the self, then tantric union can occur between them. What this means is that through exchanging energy with one another, each person will facilitate for the other greater union with the Divine Essence. Two people then become mirrors of the infinite spirit for each other and a divine romance transpires.

The heart of tantra is when you are attuned to the divinity within yourself while recognizing it within another. When that happens, there is a direct knowing that goes beyond thinking or speaking. Being totally present with the infinite spirit within yourself while simultaneously attuning to that essence within another being, the dimensions of time and space are transcended and each person is transported into the heart of the creator. To lose one's self in the eternity of the moment with another soul is the experience that makes lifetimes worth living for.

The Tantric Twin Crystals that are best suited for use with another person are those which have both of the terminations at equal height. It is even better if at least one of the faces on each crystal share the same angles. For example, if there were triangles or seven-sided configurations on each of the individual terminations, the effects would be amplified. Tantric Twin Crystals that manifest fluorescent rainbows are also ideal to work with to create stronger soul bonding with another person.

The next stage in tantra is finding that state of unity with all people and all things. This does not mean that the other person or thing is necessarily in the same state of consciousness as you are. What it does imply however, is that through the absolute connection with the Divine Essence, unity is found in all other forms originating from that same primal source. This could apply to a musician with music, an artist with art, an outdoors person with nature, a teacher with a student, a mother with her child, business partners, or any unlimited number of relationships that can occur in life. Once the primary relationship with source is established, it is only a matter of time until a tantric experience with life itself occurs.

The Tantric Twins that can be used in this type of general unification in relationships can be those which have the terminations ending at different heights. Even better are Tantric Twin Crystals that have each crystal differentiating with individual characteristics and purposes, such as a Transmitter Crystal joining together with a Tabbie (see *Crystal Healing*, Vol. II, pages 111-119, and *Crystal Enlightenment*, Vol. I, pages 62-64).

REDEFINING RIGHT RELATIONSHIP

The way that we interrelate obviously needs to be recreated if we are to enjoy peace upon this planet. On a global scale we do not yet 'love our international neighbors as ourselves.' Perhaps it is because we do not know how to love ourselves completely, so how can it be possible to truly love anything which exists outside of us? The established systems in the world encourage competition and everyone, consciously or subconsciously, tries to prove themselves better than others. This competitive pattern widens the chasm of separation and is but a reflection of the alienation that exists within our own souls. The bottom line is that we have become separate from our source so of course that state of being will manifest itself in all of our relationships, from the most personal to the internationally political.

The Tantric Twins

Another expression of source-separateness can be witnessed in the endless search to find security outside of ourselves, i.e., with other people. Those involved in relationships often depend on another person to feel loved and worthy of love. The deep void that exists within us constantly turns our attention outward, towards our partners, to fill the internal vacancy. This emptiness exists only because we have become estranged from our source. This is one of the main reasons that sexual promiscuity dominates the western world. For a brief moment we may find the temporary union of physical bodies, but unless mergence has occurred on personal inner realms, sexual encounters often leave us feeling more alone and longing for still greater fusion.

It is necessary for each person to dive into the black hole of their aloneness in order to break the bonds of illusion rooted in false securities. We have to be willing to look straight into the mirror of the soul to find the only place where true personal safety and stability abides. This can be a terrifying journey to undertake. It means that all of the old ways that we have temporarily secured ourselves in roles and relationships will be tested against the touchstone of source. It takes courage to look into the mirror of the soul and alter ourselves, as well as our relationships, in order to come into a greater sense of self-security and emotional self-sufficiency. Only by going into the very core of that aloneness is it possible to align with the essence of life itself. But, this is the only way to never, ever again feel alone or lonely.

Union with that source space takes us beyond identifying solely with the body, the mind, the e-motions, the personality and ego, the earth, the galaxy, or time and space. It even takes us beyond identification with our souls and into intimate connection with that indefinable, intangible essence of life. Only there can we find true security since the Divine Essence within us is the only thing that we can really depend on throughout eternity. Anything less than an attuned relationship with that Divine Essence is doomed to create an eventual sense of aloneness. In reality, everything less than that, at some point, will go poof and disappear.

The first phase in developing 'right relationship' then means that we take the courage to explore our inner sense of separation and fill the void with security in source. The second phase naturally follows as that empty space is nurtured and impregnated with the incredible unconditional love that springs forth from that essence. Having a firm inner foundation of security and self-love, we will no longer need to seek outside of ourselves for what can never really be found. Then, and only then, is it possible to develop 'right relationship' with others.

At this point, it can only be speculated as to how relationships will actually evolve once we have established the essentials of 'right relationship. ' What we can be sure of however, is that they will have certain characteristics that are required for all successful short or long term encounters. Greater vulnerability will no doubt be just one of the many natural outcomes of personal security and self-love. If there is fear of being hurt or rejected, we hide our true feelings, wear a false mask, put up a shield, and create emotional barriers. When inner self-security exists, we will automatically want to share ourselves honestly, openly and full-heartedly. Honest expression creates an atmosphere where nonjudgement and trust can exist. Trust leads to greater communication and unity. When these virtues are present in a relationship, a rare and wonderful love can be shared. This exquisite quality of love will inspire, honor, and support whatever changes need to occur within the relationship that will take each party into fuller expression of their Divine Essence. Commitment to this kind of unconditional love will be the ground upon which the marriages of the future can flower and the new communities will be birthed.

WORKING WITH THE TANTRIC TWINS

The Tantric Twins are crystalline entities that transmit the reality of unity. By holding them, meditating with them, sleeping with them, or just having them around, greater unification starts to take place. This could mean greater mergence of the self with source in private use, or they can be used while working with another person to create a closer connection. The Tantric Twins are wonderful marriage counselors and can be held by each party while openly communicating about relationship issues or disturbances. As interpersonal balance is restored, the Tantric Twins will begin to relay the secrets of soul partnership, transmitting the teachings on how it is possible to merge with another without losing identity or giving up personal power. While using the Tantric Twins in this way it is of added benefit to stroke one of the faces of the crystal with the index finger. The index finger channels the energies of the planet Jupiter which will relay greater wisdom into communication.

Another excellent use for the Tantric Twins is in the balancing of conflicting relationships that may or may not be so personally related. These types of relationships can include boss-employee, artist-manager, brother-sister, parent-child, friend-friend, or any other number of inter-personal encounters. If friction or discord should arise, try to work with your Tantric Twin crystal before reacting to the situation and alienating yourself from the other person. There are always solutions that can be found and the Tantric Twins will greatly assist you in discovering ways to resolve disagreements. While thinking of the other person and the situation, first hold the crystal in your left hand and become receptive to mutual resolution. Then put the crystal to your heart and allow yourself to feel genuine love for the person involved. Finally, place the crystal to the third eye and be open to receive the wisdom that will allow you to respond in 'right relationship' to the person and the circumstance.

You may also want to place that crystal in a special place or carry it with you while you openly, lovingly, and honestly communicate with the other person what is in your heart and on your mind. If the other person is not available for communication (or is deceased), program the crystal for right relationship to evolve and place it on an altar that you create especially for this purpose. (For information on how to program crystals see *Crystal Enlightenment*, Vol. I, pages 23-25). Allow that Tantric Twin crystal to stay in that special environment while the energies go to work to create balance and harmony. Leave it there until the desired result is achieved. When programming crystals that involve another person it is important to only place the person and the situation in the light of 'right relationship.' Do not project into the crystal your opinions on how the other person needs to change in order to meet your expectations. Instead, set an environment where light and love will be shed on the situation, for the betterment of all concerned, and let the energies of the Tantric Twins do the rest.

TANTRIC INITIATIONS

When working with the various phases of union that the Tantric Twin Crystals facilitate, a very powerful initiation can be preformed. This initiation can be practiced privately when fulfilling the soul's longing for fusion with source, or it can also be practiced with a loved one when seeking soul level union. Several crystalline energies are used in this initiation. Needed is one Black Obsidian Ball, at least four Rose Quartz stones, a Window Crystal, and a Tantric Twin Crystal for each participant. (See *Crystal Enlightenment*, Vol. I and *Crystal Healing*, Vol. II for the specific effects of the other crystals used). Because of the powerful effects of Black Obsidian upon the subconscious mind, it is mandatory before practicing this initiation that *Crystal Enlightenment,* Vol. I, pages 93-100 be studied and the full knowledge of working with Black Obsidian be understood.

Prepare the environment by cleaning, lighting candles and incense, etc., and securing your privacy by possibly taking the phone off the hook and leaving a 'Do Not Disturb' sign on the door. Sit in an easy cross-legged sitting position with the spine straight and place the Black Obsidian Ball in front of you on a stand or table, preferably elevated to eye level. Surround it with at least four Rose Quartz stones (eight stones would be even better). In the left hand hold the Window Crystal and place the diamond face to the third eye center. In the right hand hold the Tantric Twin Crystal at the heart center. If two people are working together, each one will hold the appropriate crystals in the hands at the heart and brow while sitting directly across from one another. The Obsidian Ball surrounded by Rose Quartz will be in-between the tantric partners.

Begin by sitting in silence with the eyes closed and call upon guidance and protection. (For more specific information on how to do this read page 30 in *Crystal Healing,* Vol. II). Then open the eyes and gaze into the Black Obsidian Ball while taking the courage necessary to dive into the depths of your sense of aloneness. Know that the Rose Quartz is there to soften the process as you face the fear of the unknown, of death, of abandonment, betrayal, rejection, or loss. The Rose Quartz will enable the inner security of self-love and personal identification with source to be seeded in the places where primal fears have been rooted for lifetimes. The Window Crystal at the third eye enables the wisdom of the soul to be accessed while in the process of clearing the subconscious and conscious minds of fear-based patterns. The Tantric Twin Crystal at the heart center allows the new energy of peaceful union to be transmitted into the depths of the heart's knowing. The Black Obsidian Ball will take you through the 'black hole' of aloneness and into the light of harmonious union. Gaze into the Obsidian Ball for seven to eleven minutes (no longer) while the darkness of fear surfaces and is dissolved.

Even if you are working with a partner, it is important that each party undergo this initial stage of the initiation before continuing with the next phase of the process. This initiation can be practiced once a week until each person feels connected and secure enough within themselves to attempt unification with the other. This Tantric initiation may bring up deep-seeded fears that require time to process. If so, be patient and do not practice this initiation again until the shadows of the surfacing fears are cleared. Know that the process is working perfectly. Feel free to carry the Rose Quartz stones, or the Window and Tantric Twin Crystals with you throughout the day and night while releasing fears and reseeding your inner security with self-love and soul wisdom.

When both partners are ready and feel the deep internal connection with their own Divine Essence, the second part of this initiation can be practiced. Set the environment and place the Obsidian Ball and Rose Quartz as before. Hold the Window Crystal to your third eye but instead of holding the Tantric Twin Crystal at your heart, reach out and with your palm flat, place it at your partner's heart chakra. Instead of staring into the Black Obsidian ball, focus your gaze directly into your partner's eyes. The eyes are the windows to the soul through which you can witness your partner's true essence. Hold the position for seven to eleven minutes while you gaze steadily, trying not to blink, into the eyes of your partner. The Tantric Twin Crystal held at your partner's heart chakra will transmit the essence of 'right relationship, ' unconditional love, and support to your beloved.

To complete this tantric initiation, lower your arms, close your eyes, and retreat into your own inner sanctums of the heart. Feel and be nurtured, by not only the love you have for yourself, but the intimate affection and warmth that the other person has just given you. Using the Tantric Twin Crystals in this way can create incredible intimacy and soul level bonding. Increased understanding and support of the other person's essence results and unconditional love finds a home in the relationship.

CHAPTER XI

THE ISIS CRYSTAL

If we search throughout planetary history in quest for our soul's true heritage, it is impossible not to give adequate attention to the wisdom offered to us by our ancient Egyptian forefathers. The great Egyptian legacy provides valuable and pertinent insight into the roots of our human origin embedded in the past.

Egypt is as old as any civilization that can be still witnessed on the planet today. Its origin has not yet been firmly established by archeologists and Egyptologists. Yet, those who have had the memory veil of time lifted from their consciousness, have experientially recognized that Egypt was founded by the surviving remnants of the Atlantian civilization.

The Egyptian kingdom has survived the tests of time down through the ages. The Greeks as well as the Romans absorbed much of their rich cultural heritage from the Egyptian empire, altering basic themes and names of Gods and Goddesses to suit their own likeness. Even today, our awe-struck attention stands witness to one of the phenomenal wonders of the world preserved from those ancient days, the Great Pyramids.

I have personally witnessed and attuned to the vast richness of this mighty empire and race of beings on several trips to this holy land. Many hours have been dedicated to personal study, meditation, and remembrance in the most ancient healing temples in the world, that of Hathor at Dendera, and of Isis on the Island of Philae. Based upon my experience at these holy shrines I have gathered the knowledge that I am now pleased to offer to you. But, before I present to you the Isis Crystal it is first important that you become aware of the ancient Egyptian legend of the Goddess Isis.

Isis, in all of her glory, is the Mother of what is defined today as "Goddess. " Isis is personified as the female creative power that conceived and brought forth all living creatures. There are no legends in our written history that precede her greatness. The Healing Temple of Isis still stands in her honor. From within those sacred walls she revealed to me the secrets of her existence, which can be as a healing balm to all, whether presently incarnated into a female or male body. It is in the balancing of the emotions that the male and female sides of each person can unite. By learning perseverance and compassion, the miracle of life is recreated. Through the feminine force, the heart is nurtured and fulfilled. These attributes, which the Goddess Isis embodies, can now be transmitted to us through the Isis Crystal.

It is once again story time so sit back, relax, and enjoy as I share with you the ancient legend of Isis. As I do, allow her presence to surround and comfort you. Be open to her essence as she relays the secrets of how to activate and inte-

THE ISIS CRYSTAL

grate the Goddess force within, and how to come into personal peace with the fragile feminine emotional body.

THE ANCIENT LEGEND OF ISIS

There are many creation stories found in Egyptian legends but they all agree that RA was the mighty source of all life whose symbol became the sun. His first creation was Shu, the god of Air, and the second Tefenet, goddess of moisture. Shu and Tefenet shared great love and before long Tefenet gave birth to twins. The younger was Nut, goddess of the sky and the elder was Geb, god of the earth. Geb and his beautiful sister Nut found great love, and as the earth and the sky merged together, birth was given to Osiris. After a great deal of pain Nut bore a second son, whose name was Set. Shortly afterwards Nut gave birth to Isis and Nephthys to serve as the female counterparts to Osiris and Set.

Osiris was born with a crown on his head and being noble and generous was destined for greatness. Set was born with the savage head of a beast and was greedy, jealous and cruel. Set resented Osiris for being created first for he knew the eldest son would inherit the throne of Ra upon the earth. Isis was brave and embodied great magical powers while Nephthys personified the virtues of loyalty and gentleness.

Ra and his children Shu and Tefenet, his grandchildren Geb and Nut, and his great grandchildren Osiris, Isis, Set and Nephthys are honored as the nine great gods and goddesses and are known as the Ennead. Ra continued his creation and called into existence many other gods and goddesses. He furnished the sky above the earth with spirits and the space below it with lesser deities and demons. He then created man and woman, the homeland of Egypt, The Nile, the seasons, the animals, and plants.

The Isis Crystal

Osiris and Isis loved each other very much and were wedded in partnership. Nephthys and Set mated, even though the gentle and loving nature of Nephthys was never in alignment with the selfish animal nature of Set. In time, Ra ordered Osiris and Isis to be the rulers of Egypt. Osiris was a kind and wise ruler and taught the people how to worship the gods, live in an orderly way, and grow crops. Set brewed with jealousy and planned to seize the throne of Egypt. Isis had never trusted Set and sought to protect her husband from his treachery.

Set pretended to be appeased but in secrecy he began to plot against his brother. Finding a group of greedy men to help him, Set waited patiently until his chance finally came. At last he was invited to a banquet at his brother's palace on a night when he knew Isis would be away.

At the banquet Set began to speak about a splendid chest that had just been made for him out of the finest wood and sent for it. While everyone was admiring the workmanship of the chest, Set promised to give it to any man who could fit exactly into it. Of course no one could exactly fit into the chest for it had been designed and constructed by Set to especially fit Osiris's specific proportions. When Osiris jokingly took his turn and got into the chest the lid was slammed and bolted down. While the innocent guests were held back by the conspirators, Set sealed the chest with molten lead and Osiris suffocated.

The chest had become Osiris's coffin. It was carried through the night to the bank of one of the Nile's many branches where it was thrown into the water, with the intent that it would drift out to the sea and be forever lost. Set then announced the sudden death of his brother and proclaimed himself the new ruler of Egypt.

When Isis returned and heard the horrifying news about her beloved, she was half mad with grief and disbelief that such a terrible thing could happen. Being unable to bear the pain of her own feelings she fled the kingdom.

It was at this time that Isis, the great ruler and goddess of Egypt, fell into a deep pit of emotional despair that only those know who have had a dearly beloved unjustly murdered. How could she, the first created Goddess, and her kind and noble husband Osiris, meet such a terrible end? Unable to make sense of her life or of the horrible fate that had befallen them, she sought refuge on the Island of Algikia where she sank into a deep dark depression. It was there that Hathor, the goddess of love and nurturing came to Isis, and feeling her agony, offered her solace. Isis rested her head on the bosom of Hathor and received deep understanding, nurturing and love. Having drawn great strength from united sisterhood with Hathor, Isis regained her personal power and was able then to restrengthen and center herself, gain her composure, and consolidate her forces.

Fortified with her fierce determination, Isis searched for the body of her murdered husband and followed rumors of his whereabouts for a very long time. Refusing to give up, she finally found the chest inside the trunk of a miraculous tree. This great tree had suddenly sprang up overnight on the seashore when the coffin of Osiris had drifted ashore and empowered its sapling roots. With an act of magic Isis removed the chest from the tree and with the help of friends the coffin was relocated to a desolate place. Isis then unsealed the lid to find that the body of Osiris had not decayed and he appeared to merely be sleeping. Isis wept bitterly as she embraced Osiris lovingly.

One night as Isis slept, Set came hunting in the marshes where she hid and found the coffin. He recognized the chest at once and was afraid of Isis's power to restore Osiris. Opening the coffin, the cruel god lifted out his brother's corpse and cut it up, joint by joint and scattered the pieces throughout all of Egypt, knowing Isis would never be able to find them all. When Isis discovered the empty coffin her cry of anguish was so great that it could be heard throughout all of Egypt. When her cry reached the ears of Nephthys, she rushed to help her sister. Even though Nephthys was the wife of Set, she had always been more attuned to Isis and Osiris than to her husband. So together the two sisters set out to search for the scattered pieces of Osiris's body.

For many long, sad years, faithful Isis and gentle Nephthys wandered throughout Egypt and in every place where they found a piece of Osiris's body they set up a shrine. (Today some of those temples still stand). At last all of the pieces were found except the phallus which had been thrown into the ocean and eaten by a whale. Calling upon her uncle Thoth to aide her, Isis worked her most powerful magic and cast the greatest of her spells to make the body whole again. With their combined magic, Isis and Thoth brought Osiris back to life for one short night of love and their child, Horus, was conceived. (This act of magic and love took place at the Osirian in Abydos, one of the most ancient of all sites in Egypt.)

Then the body of Osiris truly died. But, his spirit lived on and he became deified as the King of The Dead. Osiris, having conquered death, exemplifies the fearlessness of the immortal soul for all who dwell in this transitory world. It has since been believed that when one dies they meet with Osiris, and if a truthful life has been lived upon the earth, he/she will dwell forever in his eternal kingdom.

Horus, the falcon-headed son of Isis and Osiris, was born and there are many stories of his perilous childhood and his eventual overthrow of Set, culminating in his rightful inheritance to the throne. The stories of Horus and Set exemplify the earth-old battle between good and evil, with eventual justice and right use of power.

The Crystalline Transmission

The Power Of Feminine Force

The original Temple of Isis was constructed and rebuilt for centuries on the Island of Algikia where Isis found renewed hope. That temple stands unto this day as a monument of her eternal strength and power to balance the emotional body and heal the self. This temple is now reactivated and is transmitting those energies into the earth's aura for everyone's benefit. (Note: because of the rising waters of the Aswan dam, the Temple of Isis was moved from the island of Algikia to the Island of Philae).

Isis personifies the power of self-healing, of inner strength, of determination and perseverance to meet the final goal, of the magical power to renew life, and the ultimate outcome of truth and justice. It was only through her great strength that the creation story continued and the evil forces were brought into balance. She experienced the depth of human suffering, her anguish unsurpassed in the course of human history.

In the legend of Isis we see how this great goddess entered into the emotional body, suffered great pain and overcame her ordeal. It would have been impossible for her to proceed had it not been for the love aspect of Hathor which nurtured her heart so that she could regain her strength. It was on the Island of Algikia where she came into her true power and gathered her forces for her own self-healing before she could assist her husband. This is the primary lesson that Isis has to teach us. How do you heal from the emotional, seemingly unjust, wounds that life has to offer? How do you regain your inner strength when separated from a loved one, the worst of all pains to bear? How do you heal in order to recreate life? What is the magical spell that will bring it all into perfect order?

The Isis Crystal contains the secrets to the healing that must occur if life is to be renewed and divine justice realized.

Read on and as you do, invoke within your own being the essence of that magic and know that it is possible, in this moment, to be healed of your deepest grief. Isis, in her torment, became human. She overcame. The essence of this self-healing power is embodied in a crystalline light form. Isis will now share her secrets.

THE ISIS CRYSTAL REVEALED

Once again a Master Crystal presents itself to us with at least one of the faces manifesting a specific geometric form. (The Channeling Crystal, Transmitter Crystal, and Window Crystal detailed in *Crystal Healing*, Volume II also demonstrate geometric faces). The angular construct of the Isis face is defined and exact when examining the natural facets of the six-sided Quartz crystal. What we are looking for is a five-sided face in the front of the crystal. As with the Channeling Crystal (see *Crystal Healing*, Vol. II, page 101) the Isis Crystal will obviously have a front and a back side with the five-sided face being in the front.

The way in which the five angles form in the Isis Crystal is unique. There is a base line which connects to two lines which rise at slightly extended angles only to meet with two longer angles which rise to meet at a perfect point. As in all of the Master Crystals with specific geometric angles, the more symmetry between the opposing sides, the more balanced the crystal's energies will be. In other words, an ideal Isis Crystal is one in which the lines extending from the base, as well as the two forming the point, are of equal length. If so, the crystal will contain greater personal balance. (See photo).

The Crystalline Transmission

Geometric Significance

From the base line of the Isis Crystal rise two pairs of lines that reach eventual completion in a culminating point. As is the case when dealing with two of anything, we are usually contending with polarity, with two opposite sides. The Isis Crystal has a very special way of balancing these forces, which are prevalent everywhere in our world, whether dealing with day and night, male or female, heart and mind, or sadness and joy. The Isis Crystal unites these seemingly opposing aspects in a way that brings recognition, balance, harmony and completion to each side.

The two lower lines represent the contradictory forces that life offers for experiential growth upon the earth. They are held firm by the base line which symbolizes the physical plane dimension. The two upper lines meeting at a common point provides us with the secret for unification. It is only when we unite the opposing aspects within ourselves into a complimentary whole that the world will reflect back to us that unified reality. The Isis Crystal is unique in that the five-sided face has managed to unite the polarity forces into a whole, rescuing the opposites from a world of duality. The Isis Crystal is a powerful healing tool that transmits the knowledge of how to combine the seemingly opposite forces of life and death, sickness and health, and pain and joy. In doing so, a state of wholeness is created that is inclusive of embracing all the elements of creation.

To give an example of the idea of polarities uniting let me refer back to The Temple of Isis. There is a shrine in that ancient temple that is specifically dedicated to Hathor. Hathor is the sister aspect to Isis which provided the nurturing love force that was an essential factor in her self-healing process. Also located in the Temple of Isis is a shrine that is dedicated to Imhotep, who is the master architect that designed and erected the first pyramid. Imhotep was not a pharaoh yet his genius as an astronomer, doctor, architect and high priest was acknowledged by all and led to his deification equaling that of a pharaoh, or God-King, Son of Ra. Here in the Temple of Isis we find homage made to both the genius of the mind through Imhotep and the nurturing love force through Hathor. In our own healing process we need both the clarity and attunement of the mind, which would be the male aspect, as well as the caring of the heart, which is feminine. In order to heal the deep seeded emotional wounds that inhibit our wholeness, each of us must balance the forces of heart and mind, of male and female within ourselves. The Isis Crystal represents not only that balance, but is a symbol of the new wholeness that evolves when forces that appear to be contradictory join together in complementary unison.

Numerological Symbology

The significance of the number five in the Isis Crystal is not to be overlooked. Numerologically speaking, the number five represents the physical plane reality. We have five fingers on each hand, five toes on each foot, and five physical senses with which to perceive the material world. If we add the extremities of the body we have two arms, two legs and the head equalling the number five. Five is the number of the human soul as it enters into the realm of polarity to experience each aspect of the creation within the limitations of the five senses.

The number five evolves into the number six which represents family and social responsibility, service, love, compassion, healing, and the sixth sense of intuition. Six is the inner knowing through which the perceptions of the five senses become spiritualized. The great challenge that number five offers is that of embracing life in its wholeness instead of being limited by the perceptions of the five senses. Five signifies the mediation between opposite forces, which requires spiritual understanding and proper judgment of events.

Five represents freedom through change. It is the pivotal point in the cycle between one and ten when the soul, now encased in flesh in a polarity reality, makes a conscious choice concerning how to live life. One of the key phrases related to the number five is "freedom through change." Change in this context indicates two things. Firstly it means to make conscious choices concerning chosen changes in attitude and personal life-style. It also means a change in the way in which reality has been perceived for thousands of years, with inherited concepts of separation and duality. The choice is to relate to the whole which comprises all of the parts. This willingness to change enables greater understanding of the divine plan to develop. The number five represents the conscious decision to live life by the spiritual laws instead of being limited by the physical plane mandates. Had Isis merely accepted the death of her husband and not had the courage to try to change the situation, she would have been stranded in her human misery forever. Had she accepted that death was the end of life for Osiris, her son Horus, bringer of light and justice, would have never been conceived. Isis's willingness and courage to change her predicament was an essential factor in her self-healing process and the fulfillment of her destiny.

The Isis Crystal, also referred to as The Goddess Crystal, demonstrates how to spiritually unite the elements of polarity. The configuration of the five angles reach perfect completion in the culminating point, showing the possibility for mental and emotional balance in the material world. The five in relation to the Isis Crystal symbolizes all of the experiences that one must go through in life to contact, trust, and identify with intuitive knowing, with the whole. The completion point in the five-sided geometric face represents total attunement with the unifying soul source, the mental understanding of what life's lessons are, and the heart's acceptance and self-healing through the power of love. This mastery of the number five, of our physical senses, is something that we all must accomplish while in human form. Within the Isis Crystal is contained the secrets to that mastery enabling each individual to overcome the depths of human emotional suffering by transmitting the essence of understanding and comfort into all of life's trials and tribulations.

PERSONAL USES FOR THE ISIS CRYSTAL

The Isis Crystal encourages the integration of spiritual substance into the emotional body. Our emotional bodies were designed to experience and express the glory of spirit. But instead, we more commonly experience uncontrolled e-motions instead of feelings. E-motions are feelings that are out of alignment with spirit, therefore creating their own 'motion.' Feelings are the true experience of spirit as expressed through the heart chakra and into the physical world. By balancing the e-motions, the Isis Crystal facilitates the true experience and expression of spiritual 'feeling.'

This Goddess Crystal is not just for women. It is also very potent for men who are daring to take the courage to develop their feeling-feminine side, of integrating their emotions, and developing their intuition. It is also very effective for children (or adult-children) in the development of emotional stability. Hypersensitive people often have wounded emotional bodies because they over-identify with the sufferings of others. The Isis Crystal is extremely useful for these 'sensitives.' It will assist them in gaining a broader perspective and greater understanding. This will calm the mind which in turn will serve to balance the emotional body. Place the Isis Crystal at the third eye and/or at the heart center as needed to transmit greater understanding and balance into these chakras. Use in meditation, wear, or carry when focussing on the attributes of Isis and developing these virtues.

Many of the souls who are presently incarnating onto the earth plane are highly evolved and sensitive beings. Many children are expressing advanced degrees of psychic awareness and 'spiritual feeling'. The Isis Crystal is an excellent friend to these beings who are now coming into physical bodies with their minds and hearts totally open. The Isis Crystal will serve to protect these beautiful young people as they adjust to a world that inhabits human suffering. If worn in a pouch around the neck, carried in pockets, or slept with, the nurturing powers of Mother Isis will assist these children to remain steady and balanced while embodying the human form.

In a time when the earth is severely suffering with AIDS, cancer and a myriad other forms of dis-ease, the Isis Crystal can be of great comfort to those in the death and dying process. Through the balancing aspect of the five-sided Isis face, the polarity of life and death gains greater dimension and perspective. The Isis Crystal is an excellent companion to people who are in life transition and preparing to leave the present incarnation. In these situations keep the crystal close to the person in transition, on the bed stand, under the pillow, or if possible held in the hand. The Isis Crystal is also an empathic compassionate friend to those who are left to mourn the loss of loved ones. As Isis personally experienced the depth of human suffering and loss, She also knows how to heal and overcome that pain through love and understanding. The powerful presence of Isis emanates from this crystal and is of great service in death situations for all concerned. Carry this nurturing presence, wear, meditate with, or place on the third eye or heart center when calling upon the power of Isis to assist in overcoming the burdens inherent in the physical death ordeal. It is a crystal that allows the immortal essence of the soul (Osiris) to be contacted. In so doing, great comfort is found.

The Isis Crystal

The Isis Crystal is the most effective to use for personal self-healing after suffering the loss of a loved one, whether that person physically died or is simply no longer present in your life. It is the remedy for the 'broken heart.' The essential power of Isis lies in the fact that she sought sanctuary on the Island of Algikia and healed her wounded emotional body before she could continue her mission. This ability to retreat into the inner sanctums of the heart and rejuvenate the love force is transmitted through this crystal's geometric construct. The Isis Crystal also provides the vital healing balm necessary to nurse emotional wounds back to health so they do not inhibit the flow of spiritual 'feeling.'

The Isis Crystal can also be used to retrace old heartaches that may have occurred in the recent or distant past that have left unhealed injury to the heart chakra. Through committed use with the Isis Crystal, parts of the heart that have been deadened by the pain and sorrow of unfulfilled relationships can be renurtured back to an emotional state of well being. To use the Isis Crystal in this way, please refer to techniques and stone layouts described in *Crystal Healing*, Vol. II. Use the Isis Crystal, face up at the third eye (along with Gem Silica and Azurite) to recall into vivid remembrance the situations that need healing. Then place the Isis face downward on the heart chakra (along with Rose Quartz, Green Aventurine and Dioptase) to usher in renewed strength and comfort. The balanced five-sided face of the Isis Crystal assists one in learning the art of self-healing in times, present or past, of sorrow, grief, anger or frustration.

The Isis Crystal makes the perfect meditation comrade in any of the above situations. It is best attuned to by holding the crystal face up in the palm of the right hand while gently rubbing the thumb of the left hand across the Isis face from the base line up to the completion point. You may either close your eyes or watch the motion as you focus your attention on emotional balance, comfort and inner strength. Be prepared to learn ways in which you can use your own magic to recreate your life in a way that will bring greater peace and joy.

Another powerful meditation that can be done with the Isis Crystal is accomplished by staring directly into the 'Face of Isis' as you would with a Window Crystal (See *Crystal Healing*, Vol. II, pages 121-128). The five-sided face actually resembles a temple. As you gaze into the crystalline sanctuary of Isis your consciousness will enter into a realm of balance and harmony. Gaze into the Temple of Isis until you get a secure sense of what it 'feels' like to be completely emotionally balanced. Then gently close your eyes and place the Isis face next on the heart chakra to transmit that feeling into the inner sanctums of your own being. You may repeat this process as many times as is necessary to build the crystalline bridge of emotional health from the Isis Crystal into your own inner makeup. If this meditation is practiced with sincerity every day, deep and profound healing can occur, renewing the heart for greater reception and expression of love.

THE HATHORIAN ASPECT

Isis is the female creative power out of whose womb new Osirian life rises after death. Isis generally represents the determination of will to overcome the presence of evil and the fearlessness to stand for the truth, to right the wrong, and to courageously say "NO!" to the forces that would take advantage of, rape, humiliate and destroy goodness. Her soul-sister Hathor demonstrates the ability to bring the emotional body into balance through the healing power of love. Hathor is represented by the cow, that which nurtures, and is known as the Goddess of celebration, joy, love making, dance, music, gaiety, and art. In Egyptian legend, as well as in the ancient hieroglyphics, these two powerful Goddesses are often interchanged and sometimes seen as one and the same entity. Isis fuses easily and indistinguishably into Hathor. In some legends Hathor is older than Isis, yet in others she is born out of her. Therefore it is impossible to talk about Isis without giving ample credit to her twin-soul sister, Hathor. In studying the remains of the faces of Hathor at the powerful healing Temple of Isis, the Hathorian attributes are revealed, which when understood, can endow each one of us with the healing power of unconditional love.

The Face Of Hathor

The most striking impression one receives from meditation upon these ancient Goddess representations is one of inner peace and contentment. When looking into Hathor's eyes, they seem sad yet wide with wonder, as if she views the entire span of human suffering. She witnesses the pain and the wounds suffered by the emotional body, yet also sees the inherent beauty of life, in all of its aspects. Her ears are large and outstretched as she listens in compassion to the cries of humanity. She hears both the cries of joy and sorrow. Yet Hathor instinctively knows that all the sounds together create the symphonic music of life, which composes the eternal song of God. Hathor's mouth is slightly upturned as she expresses the inner smile of contentment. This countenance displays a peace that can only be found when life is embraced in all of its aspects. On her long graceful neck is a beaded necklace, further exemplifying the extraordinary beauty that life contains in all of its myriad expressions.

When Hathor nurtured Isis back to emotional health after she had suffered the worst of life's travesties, she must have awakened in her the ability to see and know life's beauty in the midst of suffering. This is the self-healing gift of the Isis Crystal. How do you embrace life in its fullness, gain, and grow even from the pain? How do you see the ever present beauty of creation even when life presents the greatest challenges and obstacles? How do you take the worst thing that could possibly happen, such as having your dearly beloved husband cut up joint by joint, and balance it with life's continuing presence, find your own personal peace, and heal?

The Isis Crystal, imbued with the Hathorian power of compassion, will bring cosmic perception into the heart chakra. In so doing, a new state of being will evolve that is capable of knowing true love. With the healing of the emotional body comes the balance between the mind and the heart. This is essential in order to develop the intelligence of the heart and the spiritual 'feeling nature.' Only then can it truly be known that all is well in the universe, can deep inner peace be found, and will enrichment be gained from the wholeness of life's experiences. With the powerful crystalline transmissions emanating from the Isis Crystal, we too can develop the eyes to see beauty in everything, the ears to hear the music of life in all of its rhythms, and the contented smile of inner knowing.

With this understanding in mind, the five-sided Isis face takes on a higher dimension of meaning. The base line then forms the foundation of fearlessness and the courage to go into the darkened areas of one's own heart. The two slanted lines rising from the base signify the eyes that see with wisdom and the ears that simultaneously hear the beautiful music of life. The two lines rising to the culmination point relate to the profound understanding of a contented mind and the self-healing comfort of a heart that beats in rhythm with creation. The completion point is the deep peace that is found when this balance occurs. This point of completion is the unshakable understanding that creation is more than singular lifetimes, of earthly processes, and unmeaningful occurrences. It is the point of unification where the soul accepts the natural cycles of life on earth

and in so doing, finds peace through 'know'ledge of a far
greater truth.

CHAPTER XII
THE CATHEDRAL LIGHTBRARIES

At the dawn of every two thousand year cycle, the great masters, both physical and nonphysical, gather to set a new frequency of consciousness for the next coming age. As the Age of Aries began, Moses journeyed to the top of Mount Sinai and received the written law of God which was then given to the people. When the Age of Pisces commenced, Jesus the Christ appeared upon the earth to teach the law of love; his life served as a living example of human spiritual potential. Now, as we enter into the Golden Age of Aquarius, it is possible for those same laws of God to be written upon the fabric of our hearts and for the light of love to be embodied by humanity.

In this vital transition period between the Piscean and the Aquarian Ages, the Cathedral Lightbraries have reappeared. They act as beacon stations through which the universal masters can relay to open hearts and minds specific information that is pertinent to the New Age. If properly used, the Cathedral Lightbraries can be programmed with a new pattern of thought that will establish and maintain a frequency of consciousness for the next two thousand years. Once programmed, these crystals are capable of transmitting frequencies that vibrate in accordance with the universal mind.

Some of the Cathedral Lightbraries now appearing on the surface of the earth were once used in this very same way in the ancient days of Lemuria. During that time, the Lemurian Elders worked in harmony with their non-physical comrades to create a pattern of thought that would align the universal mind to their civilization in that particular era. It is once again time to reprogram these crystals to meet the needs of a new tomorrow. Groups of dedicated and committed people will be attracted to the Cathedral Lightbraries in order to receive the new wave of consciousness and to program these specialized crystals with premeditated intentions of a better world.

THE GATHERING OF FORCES

The name 'Cathedral Lightbrary' represents both a place where God is acknowledged (a cathedral) as well as a site of knowledge and learning (a library). God is usually experienced with the heart or the intuitive sense and learning generally occurs with the mind and the intellect. The Cathedral Lightbraries are a place where like minded people can jointly balance their intuitive sense of inner knowing with pure intellect. As mental equilibrium occurs in this way, the Causal Chakra is activated and the wisdom of the soul can take tangible form in thoughts that the mind is capable of understanding.

Cathedrals, as well as libraries, can be somewhat impersonal in that they exist to serve whoever may come into them.

But, all of those who enter into such places have a common purpose or goal, i.e. to learn and/or to relate to God. The Cathedral Lightbraries combine the attributes of both places and are destined to gather people around them who have common intentions and goals. The common denominator among all of the people who will consciously work with these crystals will be their shared attunement to the light, the love of God, and the quest for greater truth and 'know'ledge.

In a sense, a Cathedral Lightbrary is like a learned professor or an enlightened master around whom many people gather in order to learn. This Master Crystal establishes the order, sets the tone of the teaching, and determines the way in which specific information will be disseminated. The responsibility of those who come to learn is to decide what subject matter they want to be taught. Once clear intention is set forth by the participants, they can then open their minds to receive the information that the crystal will transmit.

RECOGNIZING CATHEDRAL LIGHTBRARIES

The Cathedral Lightbraries are quartz crystals that appear as if they are made up of many parts. In fact, each part is a single crystal that is similar or practically identical to the others. These individual portions may look like they have been joined together or may even seem to penetrate one another. They are all bonded to a larger 'mother' crystal which forms a single termination. The Cathedral Lightbraries can appear complex in their varied shapes, as groups of many individually recognizable crystals merge in numerous formations. Though they are difficult to describe in written words, once seen, The Cathedral Lightbraries are easy to recognize.

In mineralogical terms, the appearance of one large crystal with many smaller crystals contacting and interpenetrating one another, is caused by a phenomenon called 'twinning. ' In the case of Cathedral Lightbraries, a double spiral rotation occurs within the internal make up of the crystal producing the steps and offsets along its sides and top. This double spiraling motion in the Cathedral Lightbraries is exactly what makes them susceptible to both receiving universal frequencies as well as being receptive to human thought forms.

The Cathedral Lightbraries can be mistaken for Elestials (see *Crystal Healing*, Vol. II, pages 129-141), in that both display individual smaller crystals that are tightly joined to a larger crystalline structure. The Cathedral Lightbraries, however, can be distinguished by the following characteristics. First, they are unified into one singly terminated crystal, whereas Elestials may have several terminated points on a single piece, may be single terminated, or may not have any terminated apexes. Elestials are etched and layered with markings, exposing layer upon layer of inner dimension within the body of the crystal. The Cathedral Lightbraries may reveal some etching, but they do not display deeply ingrained layers in the internal make up of the crystal. The energies of the Elestials are focussed inward as they assist people in accessing personal truth by taking them deep within the core of their own beings. The energies in the Cathedral Lightbraries project outwards as they stand open to receive the impressions of the universal mind as well as collective human thought forms. The Elestials may be as small as one quarter inch and as large as three feet in length or width, whereas the Cathedral Lightbraries are usually at least six inches in length and two to three inches wide. Elestials are generally either clear or smoky in color and vary in luster, while the Cathedral Lightbraries can be clear, smoky, or citrine and are usually exceptionally transparent.

THE COSMIC CRYSTALLINE COMPUTER

In ways, the Cathedral Lightbraries are also similar to the Record Keepers and the Earthkeepers in that they, too, are capable of being programmed and relaying information. But again, the Lightbraries are unique and differ both in the way in which they are programmed as well as the types of energies that they are receptive to and can project. The Record Keepers, (see *Crystal Enlightenment*, Vol. I, pages 65-68) are personally oriented and can be used by individuals to receive information that has been held in safe keeping for thousands of years. They may also contain specific information for an individual whose presence literally manifests the records on the crystal. The giant Earthkeepers (see *Crystal Healing*, Vol. II, pages 155-164) are planetarily oriented and have recorded specific information concerning the history of the earth and the evolution of the human species. The Cathedral Lightbraries are universally oriented and have the amazing ability to synchronize with universal frequencies. Once programmed, they have the potential to not only embody those vibrations but to translate them into our thinking modes.

In short, the Cathedral Lightbraries, if properly programmed, can contain the sacred knowledge written in the language of light. This universal knowledge is known as the 'akasha. ' It is upon these 'akashic records' where every thought, word, and deed of every living thing throughout time has been registered. The Cathedral Lightbraries have the innate ability to differentiate and gather only those thought-forms that are in alignment with the supreme intelligence, or mind of God. Therefore, these Lightbraries are destined to collect the refined essence of primal substance and convert it into a language that the human mind is capable of grasping.

With very little imagination the extensions protruding upon a Cathedral Lightbrary could appear to be crystalline data banks. Indeed, that is just what they are. The individual crystals forming upon the body of the 'mother' are the data banks which gather the omniscient forces of universal knowledge. These data banks are open, clear, and unprogrammed until conscious thoughts and intentions are projected into them. It is very similar to the way that a computer works in our day and age. Until the computer and blank disks are specifically programmed with facts, figures, documents, charts, etc., they remain void of information.

The specific requirement necessary to program the Cathedral Lightbraries is the dedicated commitment of at least two people (preferably more than two) who can merge their hearts, minds, and conscious intentions together as one. The Cathedral Lightbraries maintain absolute attunement and integrity with universal frequencies and do not lower their vibration to the level of individual mentality. Rather, the Cathedral Lightbraries challenge a group of individuals to expand awareness and merge their minds into collective cohesiveness in order to attune with the universal mind. With the prerequisite of unified group consciousness, the practitioners can then enter with clarity and unison into the 'cathedral of light.' Once the group mind has projected inside of the crystal, the participants can then harmonize with the refined frequencies of the akasha and receive profound 'know'ledge.

USING THE CATHEDRAL LIGHTBRARIES

The function of the Cathedral Lightbraries is three-fold. First, they are receptors for the pure substance of undefined thought. Secondly, they will maintain attunement to the universal mind while reformulating and redefining the conscious thoughts that a group will project into them. Finally, they will reinterpret the collective intention and project it back into the minds of the group participants in a way that will formulate their thoughts in accordance with the purity of the universal mind. In so doing, specific thought forms, ideas, and concepts are translated from the level of divine consciousness into the perceptions received by the group. It then becomes the responsibility of the group members to ground themselves, and get practical in order to follow through with their insight and manifest their goals on the physical plane.

The Cathedral Lightbraries can be used by any group of people who share the common intention of bringing the Divine Essence and the light of universal truth into human endeavors. They serve to establish a higher order in any mutually agreeable venture whether the aim is to create a healing center or new age business, to formulate harmonious interpersonal or family relations, or to develop a new structure not yet dreamed of.

For example, if a group of like-minded individuals choose to establish a new business based in spiritual integrity, they will first sit around the Cathedral Lightbrary, which will be in an upright position in the center of the circle. The group will then discern exactly what kind of venture they want to undertake and agree upon common intentions. Then, without any further expectation or forethought they will hold hands, harmonize hearts and minds, and project into the crystal to receive further insight and instruction. Once within the crystal, the individual crystalline data banks will appear as different lighted chambers inside a giant cathedral. Each individual may then enter alone into a separate chamber to receive divine perception and guidance. There will usually be very little mental activity at this time as the Causal Chakra is imprinted with impressions that will create the mental blueprint for the material manifestation of the business. The amount of time the group spends projecting into the crystal will vary depending upon the individuals' combined ability to mentally focus as well as the nature of the intention. The time period usually varies between eleven and thirty minutes and should not exceed one hour. Once everyone returns back into their physical bodies, ideas will be triggered and the way will be clear and open for creative discussion.

It is important when using the Cathedral Lightbraries in this way that the group continue to hold hands throughout the entire time while they are projecting into the inner sanctums of the crystal. This will keep everyone united, grounded, and focussed on the common purpose and intention. The discussion period afterward is also necessary in order to activate the causal impressions that have been transmitted by the crystal. In this vital communication time ideas will formulate that will enable practical realistic steps to be taken.

The programmed Cathedral Lightbrary will continue to transmit 'know'ledge and information to those committed to manifesting their goals. These crystals can then be set up in the place of business (or wherever the participants will gather) and be used as a focal point in group meetings or interactions. Once programmed, the Cathedral Lightbrary will transmit ideas and thoughts into the minds of the participants on an on going basis to aide in fulfilling the common goal. The crystal will retain the same program for long periods of time, or it can be cleansed with pure water and sunlight (see *Crystal Enlightenment*, Vol. I, page 28) and be collectively reprogrammed with other intentions.

In the not too distant future, the Cathedral Lightbraries will attract groups of individuals who are ready and willing to participate in reprogramming the various planetary structures presently existing with the consciousness of supreme intelligence. As universal energy is directed into worldly systems in this way, a new order based in truth, honesty, integrity and mutual reward can be established upon the earth.

ACCESSING THE HALL OF RECORDS

The sacred Hall of Records originally existed in ancient Egypt and was composed of mighty columns of light. It was located in a long underground hallway that extended from the feet of the Sphinx into the subterranean chamber of the Great Pyramid. Only advanced initiates, capable of attuning to the frequency of light, were allowed to enter this holy hallway and decipher the akasha recorded therein. This Hall of Records was the mightiest of lightbraries, registering upon the massive radiant columns everything that has ever, or would ever, occur throughout the eternity of the universe. Dedicated initiates, as well as high priests and priestesses would gather there, attune to the frequency of light, define their intentions, and read segments of the akashic records. There they could learn chapters of human history, witness events occurring in other times and places, or observe different dimensions of reality.

As the Egyptian Empire fell into ruin, the Hall of Records was kept hidden and secret. Only secret mystery schools retained fragments of information concerning its presence and purpose. When the Alexandria Library was burned, virtually all of the knowledge concerning this ancient lightbrary was destroyed and lost.

The Cathedral Lightbraries can potentially serve the same purpose as the columns of light in the Hall of Records. If used correctly, the blank data banks can be programmed to contain any information that has been recorded in the past or the future. With sincere group effort and dedicated common intention, 'know'ledge and wisdom can be attained that otherwise might remain permanently inaccessible to human consciousness.

To use the Cathedral Lightbraries in this way, follow the same procedure as described above but clearly define in the group mind exactly what specific information is to be attuned to. Then, holding hands, each individual within the group will simultaneously project into the cathedral of light and perceive the desired knowledge. Afterward, each member of the group should openly share whatever information he/she received. Combine all of the versions, build upon collective knowledge and experience, and together paint a colorful picture of the chapter that has just been read from the akashic records.

CHAPTER XIII

THE DEVIC TEMPLE CRYSTALS

In my opinion, the Devic Temples are among the most special of all the Master Crystals. They embody an element of pure magic and if properly used, can provide a gateway through which devas can enter into the physical plane. 'Devas' are generally defined as inner plane beings that exist in the higher astral and/or heaven worlds. Those that exist in the astral plane may be resting in between incarnations. The devas that exist in the higher heaven worlds have evolved out of the cycle of reincarnation, or they can be angelic beings that have never inhabited physical bodies. All devas are beings of light. Because they abide in higher planes of consciousness, they are not encumbered with the weight of mental or emotional strain, nor are they disillusioned by the limiting perceptions of the five senses. Some of these devas are dedicated to assisting human beings presently incarnated on the physical plane. Their aim is to facilitate spiritual unfoldment, self-realization, and guide us on the path towards our own self-mastery. When used in the right way, the Devic Temple Crystals can become temporary vehicles through which the inner plane devas can find expression and offer insight, wisdom, and blessings into our lives.

IDENTIFYING DEVA DWELLINGS

The Devic Temples are specialized quartz crystals and yet their features are less defined than any of the other Master Crystals. These crystals are usually single generators. The traits that distinguish the Devic Temples from other crystals are found by observing the inclusions within the internal world of the crystal as well as the markings upon the body and the faces. The crystals that can be used as temple sites for higher plane beings can display impressions of other worlds, temples, or most importantly, faces or outlines of beings inside of the crystal. The body of a Devic Temple Crystal may exhibit clearly defined doorways or avenues of entry. Devas can also be invoked through crystals that have ascending steps and/or lines on the body or any of the terminating facets.

Because clear quartz crystals inherently integrate the white light of the spiritual realm into the substance of the earth plane, The Devic Temples are perfect dwelling places for higher beings. The Devic Temple Crystals provide the contact point between dimensions, enabling the higher astral and/or heavenly devas easy access into the physical plane. Only the devas who are capable of merging with pure white light are able to cross the threshold between worlds and temporarily reside within the crystal temple. And when they do, communication between the inner and outer realms can be bridged. When the devas are invited into your life through these crystals, a magical presence prevails. The harmonic

THE DEVIC TEMPLE CRYSTALS

vibration of these quartz temple sites allows the veils between the worlds to be lifted and spiritual energies to infiltrate into the environment. The Devic Temple Crystals become living altars through which the masters of the inner worlds can see into the eyes, heart, and soul of the one who will meditate with the crystal.

THE NATURE OF A TRUE TEMPLE

In the incredible activity of the western world in the twentieth century, so very little time is devoted to inner reflection. And yet, it is within the inner sanctums of the self where one can find the peace that the soul deeply longs for and that the world so desperately needs. True temples are places where sincere ceremony is performed on a daily basis, creating a vortex where spiritual energy is established upon the earth plane. It is within these temples that inner reflection and communication with the self can most easily occur. Such places of God facilitate mergence with the Divine Essence. Devas often reside within true temples and offer direction and benediction to receptive hearts and minds. In ancient times many temples stood in honor of the divinity of life. Today, there are very few true temples such as this existing in the western world. However, as the dawn of the new age grows ever brighter upon the horizon, more of these holy sanctuaries will be erected. They will stand as beacons of light through which the spiritual and material realms harmonize and become one.

The inner planes exist within the material world. The astral and the heavenly realms are right here, right now, only functioning at a higher rate of vibration. The veils that exist between the varying worlds become very thin in true temples, enabling the physical and the inner worlds to be simultaneously witnessed. In such places it is easier for the higher beings on the inner planes to connect with the material world, as well as for human beings to contact the angels. When worshiping in a genuine temple embodying a high vibrational frequency, it is possible to sense, see, or feel the devas that reside there. The devas that dwell within true temples assist those who come to worship in contacting their own God-self.

The Devic Temple Crystals can serve as personal shrines through which this same phenomenon can occur. Within the hustle and bustle of twentieth century life, individual sanctuaries can be created through which devic presences can be invoked. The Devic Temples can be enshrined in such a way as to create living altars that will function as mini-models until the new age temples are built.

CREATING A LIVING ALTAR

An altar is a place where humility and reverence inspires submission to the omniscience of the Divine Essence. Altars are easily created and can be simply constructed by placing a white cloth over a table, constructed especially to suit individual taste, or elaborately built with gold and precious gems. Personal treasures such as pictures of saints, crystals, and objects of intimate spiritual meaning can be placed upon the altar as a reminder of your personal relationship with the divine. The altar that will house a Devic Temple Crystal requires special attention and several specific items in order to create an opening through which a deva can enter into the crystal.

Prior to sitting before the altar create an atmosphere that is conducive to quiet inner reflection. Purify your environment by smudging (see *Crystal Healing*, Vol. II, page 16) and letting fresh air circulate. Place a Devic Temple Crystal in the center of a clean fresh altar that has been created especially for this purpose. Devas are enchanted with the subtle essences of the earth. Therefore, the fragrance of fine incense, the intoxicating beauty of fresh flowers, and the flame from a burning white candle should be placed around the crystal to send out an invitation to the devas. It is important to make some kind of personal offering and place it upon the altar each time that you call forth a deva. This could be a special food that has been prepared, a personal healing stone, or anything that is near and dear to your heart. This act of giving will open you up to receive whatever blessings the deva might offer in return. You may also choose to aurically outline the Deva Temple Crystal with Kyanite to open up the forcefield of the crystalline temple (for further instructions read Kyanite, page 71).

Once the altar has been awakened with the fragrance of incense, the beauty of flowers, and the candle flame, sit before it and offer the gift of sound. It is most effective if you personally sing, chant, tone, or play a musical instrument. If this is not possible or if it is uncomfortable for you, soft etheric music may be played on a cassette player in the background. Then close your eyes, and go within. In the sanctity of your inner being, call forth the deva that can most easily attune to you and ask that it enter into the highly refined energies of the crystal temple. Then open your eyes and gaze into the Devic Temple Crystal. Allow your mind to remain clear and your heart to be open and receptive. If you have questions or need guidance, mentally project yourself and the situation into the Devic Temple. The solutions may reveal themselves at once, or they may not. What you can be sure of is that your prayers have been heard and will be responded to in accordance with divine will.

Once the altar has been set up it is necessary to keep it activated in order to receive the deva's energy on an on going basis. The devas can only temporarily reside within the Devic

Temple Crystal unless personal worship is maintained in front of the altar on a daily basis. The candle and incense should be lit every day, wilted flowers replaced, fresh offerings made, and meditation performed regularly. If the altar is maintained in an active state, it is much easier for the deva to enter into the crystal and become a constant presence in your life. Meditation at these personal shrines can become a healthy daily practice and can easily be incorporated into any maintenance plan.

INDIRECT ASSISTANCE

The devas that will work through the Devic Temple Crystals in this way are solely committed to assisting you in accessing the inner sanctums of your own being. The fact that you consciously set up an altar and ask for guidance provides the devas with the permission necessary to lend their assistance. However, it is unlikely that you will get to know them personally, even though it is possible. It is more likely that the relationship will be impersonal and that their guidance will be indirect. It is no longer appropriate to give personal power away to any outside force, whether it be to gurus, crystals, space beings, or inner plane beings. When working with the Devic Temple Crystals, the objective is not to hand over your responsibility to another being. The purpose and intention of the devas is to offer higher guidance and direction that will in turn assist you to go within and become more aware of your true identity and more connected to your own source. The devas are master teachers working through Master Crystals to teach self-mastery. They do not want to establish the kind of relationship that could turn into a psychic distraction.

It is true that along life's path it is possible to get lost, forget the real purpose, lose direction, and slip into material illusion. The best way to go or the right path to take is not always obvious. It is at such times that the devas can be called forth through the medium of these crystals to lend insight, direction and guidance. The devas will work indirectly, through circumstances, people, and situations, to increase your understanding so that you will be better able to make the best possible decisions regarding your life's path. They may trigger ideas through dreams that will facilitate new creations, channel healing energies, or etherically remold the energy to better serve your unfoldment. The devas are able to amplify their energies and send them out through these crystals to help clear up conditions that might otherwise require lifetimes of effort and experience.

With the intention of going within to find true identity, the devas can be invoked through the Devic Temple Crystals to assist your life in becoming increasingly easier, happier and more stable. These Master Crystals are mediums through which the Divine Essence can be expressed through sincere messengers of light onto the earth plane with integrity, wisdom, and love. The Devic Temples are receptors for only the inner plane beings that are dedicated to human evolution. They will point the way, like a direct arrow, into the very heart of God.

INNER EARTH BEINGS EMERGING

At the decline of the great civilization of Lemuria, many members of that race transformed their physical structures and entered into the realms of inner earth. Maintaining their identity as 'earthlings' they have worked diligently for the planet within the earth's inner core for thousands of years. Indeed, it is these very beings who have created so many of the crystals and minerals that have been discovered and mined in the last decade. Now, some of them are literally incarnating onto the surface of the earth in crystal bodies.

These beings are different from the devas that can be called forth into the Devic Temple Crystals. These ancient Lemurians are another breed of being altogether, and yet they vibrate at a high enough frequency where it becomes possible for them to embody a crystalline form. In this situation, any number of different crystals and stones may be the dwelling places for inner earth Lemurians. These highly refined beings will manifest themselves in a crystal or a stone in a way that will leave no doubt whether or not they are there. Sometimes a face with distinct features and rainbow eyes will be found within a crystal. Or, an entire body with explicitly defined limbs and an elaborate costume will be present, presenting no question that the crystal or stone is inhabited.

These ancient Lemurians have surfaced on the earth in pure crystalline form at this time in order to relay certain messages and transmit information that can help us now in the salvation of our planet. They have seen the rise and fall of their own civilization and have learned throughout the ages how to prevent destruction, whether it be of a race, or of an entire planet. These crystalline beings are mostly appearing in crystals and stones that are being mined in Brazil. Understandably so, since South America is one of the locations where remnants of the Lemurian Empire can be found. Brazilian quartz as well as tourmaline often provide the vehicles through which inner earth Lemurians can incarnate.

These crystalline entities will attract themselves to the people who they can best work with. Most likely, it will be those who have had lifetimes in Lemuria and perhaps have even had a close personal acquaintance with the being inhabiting the crystal. When meditated with, the Lemurian will relay to the human working with it knowledge that can be used to assist the planet in this fragile transitory period between ages. Advanced technological and scientific information may be received that can be directly applied to new inventions that will serve to preserve the environment, repair the ozone layer, or facilitate human endeavors.

If you are meant to work with an inner earth being of this kind, you will know it. Your particular profession or way of life may be the perfect medium through which the Lemurian's knowledge can be utilized. If this type of crystal is placed under the pillow, or on a night stand by the bed while sleeping, ideas may sprout up over night or information may be seeded into the dream state. If you find yourself with one of these crystals, first meditate with it, establish contact with the being inside, and let the crystal itself communicate to you the way in which it is to be used.

CHAPTER XIV
THE TIME LINK CRYSTALS

The Time Link Crystals are often mistaken for Window Crystals (see *Crystal Healing*, Vol. II, pages 121-128). This is understandable since they are very similar in appearance. The difference between the two is that a Window Crystal will display a large perfect diamond face in the center of the crystal whereas a Time Link Crystal will exhibit a parallelogram. Unless observed closely, the parallelogram is often misidentified as a diamond face and incorrectly labeled as a window.

The Time Link Crystals are abundant where true Window Crystals are more difficult to locate. Whenever there is a window or a parallelogram as one of the faces forming the termination of a crystal, a seventh facet is created which empowers the crystal with added dimension and power. There may be as many as three or four parallelograms found in one single crystal which would indicate that multi-dimensional realities can be perceived through that particular Time Link Crystal.

It seems as if the parallelogram is one of the main geometrical teachers at this point in time as both Time Link Crystals and rhomboid Calcite crystals are appearing in quantity. The ability that parallelograms have to link parallel realities is discussed in detail in Chapter Six on Calcite. Time Link Crystals can be worked with in many of the same ways as rhomboid Calcite and yet they offer their own unique and exciting expertise in linking simultaneous existences. Time Link Crystals are like bridges that the soul can travel upon in order to consciously connect with aspects of the self existing in other times and places.

The fact that two sets of parallel lines are linked together in this Master Crystal can be interpreted symbolically. One line represents the self that is presently existing. The line directly below it pertains to an aspect of the self that is existing in another time and place. The two parallel lines to either side link those aspects together and form a bridge through which the present self can commune with past or future selves.

The parallelograms that can be found in The Time Links are caused by a particular type of spiraling growth pattern within the internal make-up of the crystal. The innate molecular structure of these crystals could be likened to a spiral staircase which may turn to the left or to the right. If the parallelogram is on the right side as you face the crystal, it indicates that the spiral is spinning in a clockwise direction, or forward, and will take you into the future. If the parallelogram is on the left side as you face the crystal, the spiral is spinning counterclockwise, or backwards, and will allow you to travel into the past. If there happens to be parallelograms on both the right and left sides, a double spiral motion is in effect and time can be bridged in either direction with that particular crystal.

THE TIME LINK CRYSTAL

DISSOLVING THE MISCONCEPTION
OF LINEAR TIME

The life that we are presently living is but one facet of who we really are. Yet, being born into a physical body that is governed by the five senses, we have been conditioned to view time as a linear event with a beginning, a duration, and an end. Being programmed with this perception since birth, we have forgotten that we are actually multi-dimensional beings existing in an eternity of time. With the help of the Time Link Crystals, life can be witnessed out of linear sequence. Then, the illusion of three dimensional reality, bound in time and space, can be dissolved and time travel becomes possible. The key to traversing through time is to identify with the essence of the soul that is living each life. With the soul as a trustworthy guide, past as well as future identities can be witnessed and ancient heartaches can be healed. As the lessons of each life experience are integrated, all of our alter identities can be blended into one unified sense of self.

Up until this point in time, it has not been possible to integrate and assimilate all of the fragmented aspects of our beings. But now, as we complete this great time cycle, and with the aide of the Time Link Crystals, parts of us that have been frozen in time through trauma, pain, and misunderstanding can be freed. As we learn to relate to time in a way that includes the concept of the immortal soul, we can link all aspects of ourselves in other incarnations into the wholeness of the eternal moment. That is the purpose that the Time Link Crystals have come to serve.

RIDING THE RIBBON OF LIGHT

The parallelogram on a Time Link Crystal reflects light in a unique way. It is a crystalline representation of a ribbon of light; a code that has been programmed onto these crystals that can be tapped into in order to time travel. As you gaze into the parallelogram, you will begin to see a wave-like motion that will move up and down. Once you sense that movement, close your eyes and begin to breathe long and deep in rhythm with the wave, inhaling as it rises and exhaling as it falls. With concentration focussed at the Soul Star, allow your light body to travel upon this ribbon of white light to your chosen destination.

You may become aware of a lifetime that needs healing through your personal attunement in meditation with a Time Link Crystal. Or, these specialized crystals can be used at the third eye center in crystal healings to help lift the memory veils when a past life experience is having a direct effect upon this lifetime. They can also be used in sessions when vivid past life remembrance has occurred and it is necessary to release the patterning of pain and learn the lessons that were not possible to learn in a previous incarnation. The purpose of past life regression or future life progression is to neutralize whatever magnets exist in other existences that keep our consciousness and actions bound to the limitations of the third dimension.

Please be aware that it is not safe to use these crystals to 'time trip' and just take off to see where you might end up. When the soul body travels upon the ribbon of light it is necessary to have a consciously chosen destination and know exactly which lifetime you intend to visit. The incarnations that you choose to reconnect with will most naturally be the ones that you can give healing energy to and serve with your present insight. It is potentially dangerous, as well as a psychic sidetrack, to use these crystals to link into lifetimes that do not need your personal assistance. If these crystals are used for personal ego purposes, spiritual growth will be stunted.

When using the Time Link Crystal, you will be acting as your own spirit guide or guardian angel to other aspects of yourself in past or future incarnations. Therefore, it is also required that preparation time be spent prior to riding the ribbon of light so that you will maintain a clear connection to your source while dissolving the boundaries of time. Whether this experience is to be undertaken alone while meditating or with the assistance of a crystal healer, it is necessary to center yourself, call upon the Divine Essence, and maintain a strong connection with your identity in this life. (For more information on centering and past life therapy read *Crystal Healing*, Vol. II, Part I). It is also helpful to hold Black Tourmaline in both hands to ground and stabilize yourself following this type of time travel.

HEALING THE WOUNDS OF THE PAST

The parallelograms found on Time Link Crystals are often found next to an Isis Face (see The Isis Crystal, page 153). Since the purpose of the Isis Crystal is promote self healing, these particular crystals are the best to use when bridging into a past experience that has retained impressions of pain. This could mean an aspect of your own inner child from this life that needs nurturing or an expression of yourself that is existing in a parallel reality within a different time zone. The Time Link Crystals will first link your consciousness with your light body. Then, as your soul rides upon the ribbon of light to the chosen destination, you will be able to bond with your past self in order to communicate and transmit healing energy.

As an example of using the Time Link Crystals, I would like to relay a personal experience. When I was traveling in

The Time Link Crystals

Egypt and visiting the ancient healing temples, I became aware of several lifetimes where I had been a priestess in the temples. There was a deep sorrow that surfaced when I thought of the temples being destroyed when the Romans entered Egypt and invaded the country. In that past lifetime, I thought that the light was being destroyed and the knowledge that was contained within the temples would be lost forever. With the use of an Isis faced Time Link Crystal I traveled back and communicated to myself existing then what I now know. I relayed to the saddened priestess that nothing can ever destroy the light and that the knowledge is being resurfaced at a future time when the masses are ready to receive it. With the insight that I have now, I was able to heal the deep-seeded wounds within my being that originated thousands of years ago. My present lifetime has also been enriched through that experience as I embrace the reality that the light continues to exist in many shades and colors and will survive all of the elements of time.

There is an amazing phenomenon that occurs when using these crystals. It is as if you can literally change history and heal an aspect of yourself in the past that can only be healed if you go back and teach it what you know now, after lifetimes of experience. Not only does the present self benefit, but the past selves as well have an opportunity to reap the rewards of your accumulated experience.

The way that you will affect another aspect of yourself in a past life may be subtle. Your past self may not be willing or ready to have you enter into that life in full form, to invite you to sit right down and have a conversation. You may need to appear to your past self as a reflection in a pool of water, as a cloud, as a beam of light, or in some other subtle, unthreatening form. You may only be able to transmit a thought or plant seeds in the subconscious. It may be necessary to travel back a number of times to relay the message and nurture the seeds that you have sown. After each time, program the Time Link Crystal that you used for traveling to keep the connection with your alter self. The crystal that is worked with for each lifetime should be untouched by other people and kept on an altar or in a special place. It should also be meditated with until the simultaneous realities have merged and the past self is healed.

REAPING FUTURE REWARDS

Time Link Crystals can also be used to tune into an aspect of yourself that is existing in the future. In this case, a very special opportunity presents itself. If you can see through the eyes of a future self that is living on the earth two or three hundred years from now, you will be able to see how the planet survived these trying times. You may even be able to tap into technologies that were developed in order to save the planet from destruction. If so, that knowledge can be brought back into the present time to find the necessary solutions to preserve the environment, repair the ozone, and facilitate peace. With the aide of your future self, inventions and creations can be brought forth in this time of need that otherwise would not be thought of for hundreds of years.

Again, this is another phenomenon that Time Link Crystals facilitate. The very fact that you are able to link with a future aspect of yourself gives birth to the possibility of creating a new reality in the future as well as in the present. By taking conscious steps across the bridge of time, it is possible to manifest for the future that which is presently only a probability. It is an act of outwitting time, the greatest of fantasy stories. But who is to say that your future self isn't there in some subtle form for you now to secure its life in the year 2300?

Ingenious scientists, technicians and intellectuals will be attracted to these crystals to perform this life-preserving service for the planet. At first they may not understand why, but if their minds are open to the possibility of conscious time travel, not only will they render great assistance to the planet, their own evolution will be accelerated. These courageous persons will be capable of bringing into the present, future knowledge that will transform the earth. In so doing, they will become the legends future history will record.

EASING PHYSICAL PASSING

The Isis faced Time Link Crystals can also be effectively used and programmed for someone who is dying. The light that is reflected off of the parallelogram in a Time Link Crystal connects to the light in other dimensions. It is upon that beam of light that the soul can travel at the time of death. When a loved one is nearing death of the physical body, give him/her an Isis faced Time Link Crystal to hold, meditate with, and gaze into. As this beam of light is accessed it will help the person in transition to become familiar with his/her own light body. Then, at the moment of death, it will be much easier for the soul to identify with the Divine Essence and release physical attachments.

After death, the Time Link Crystal that was used by the dying person can be placed with the termination straight up on an altar that has been made especially for the deceased. It can be programmed with thoughts of the departed loved one finding his/her way to the light on the other side. The Time Link Crystal will literally create a beam of light that the soul, in its expanded non-physical state, can easily find and use as a guide post in the transition process.

It is of great comfort for both the dying person, as well as the one left to live in the physical world, to work with The

Time Link Crystals in this way. A conscious agreement can be made by both parties to assist the departing soul in its transition to connect with the light in the spirit world. It also eases the grief that is experienced by the survivor to know that the greatest effort is being made for the soul of the dying person. By relating to the needs of the soul, instead of the body or the personality, the survivor's suffering and great sense of loss can be comforted. As the survivor meditates with that crystal it is also possible to get a glimpse of the non-physical world and see the soul that has passed dancing in a body of light.

The less attachment there is at the moment of death to the personality, ego, loved ones, and physical possessions, the easier the transition will be. If the consciousness is identified with the light body, it will be easier for the soul to make a conscious transition, let go of the illusions of this world, and identify with the Divine Essence. If a soul is able to achieve this, the greatest of all challenges, all of life's traumas are neutralized and spiritual freedom is attained.

SECTION IV
MORE IMPORTANT
HEALING STONES

INTRODUCTION
MORE
IMPORTANT HEALING STONES

The stones that are covered in this section are ones that I have come to love and respect through my personal work with them. These stones, as well as the many others that have been previously written about in the first two volumes, are ones that have attracted themselves to me so that their healing powers could become publicly known and accepted. There are many other stones deserving this kind of attention and acknowledgment. If a stone has not been covered in this Crystal Trilogy it does not mean that it is not an important stone, but rather that it is for you to personally resonate with it in order to hear its message.

The important healing stones discussed in this section vary in color, purpose, and use. Some have just recently been discovered upon the earth and have manifested at this point in time in order to lend their special healing energies as we enter into a new decade and close a great time cycle. Some transmit soft blue rays that can assist us in building a foundation of inner peace within our own beings. Still others will serve to balance the heart and mind, ground the love force into the body, and transmute emotional pain while rejuvenating the heart's courage to love. Whatever the purpose, these stones are useful agents in the process of the Crystalline Transmission. I am sure that you will love them as much as I do.

CHAPTER XV

BLUE LACE AGATE

Blue Lace Agate reminds us of soft blue skies with wisps of gentle clouds. It hints of calmness and peaceful expression. Manifesting a light blue ray, this member of the quartz family works most effectively at the throat chakra and is specifically endowed with powers that will assist in verbal expression. Being that the color of the throat chakra is blue, there are many stones that can be worn or placed there that can be useful such as Chrysocholla, Turquoise, Larimar, Amazonite, Celestite, Gem Silica, Aquamarine and Indicolite. But, none has a more peaceful countenance than the soft presence of Blue Lace Agate.

To a large degree, we have been programmed to suppress ourselves. Fear of being harshly judged or rejected has stifled many a thought and feeling. When we do not freely express what is felt within the heart and thought with the mind, the throat chakra suffers (as well as the chest and head). Since the throat chakra is situated between the heart and the head, its purpose is to serve as a medium of expression for both our thoughts and our feelings. But, when we fail to exercise this freedom, the throat chakra can become constricted resulting in ailments such as headaches, neck and shoulder tension, tonsil and lymph infections, sore throats and thyroid problems. The worst problem of all is that once this suppressive pattern sets in, it becomes increasingly difficult to even internally acknowledge what is really being felt and/or thought. In our society, men have been especially programmed to neglect their sensitive feeling nature. Blue Lace Agate is an ideal stone for men (as well as women) who are willing and ready to express exactly what they think and feel. Placed at the throat chakra in crystal healing layouts it will greatly assist in the verbalization of thoughts and feelings, known or unknown.

Blue Lace Agate exemplifies peaceful channels of expression with its soft, gentle blue background lined with lighter bands of white. Blue Lace Agate can be carried or worn whenever you want to maintain calm, truthful verbalization. Being that its nature exudes the peace of the blue ray, this quartz agate can be placed over any part of the body that is in need of a soothing, cool, gentle energy. It is especially good for the neutralization of red energies such as anger, infections, inflammations, or fevers.

Blue Lace Agate clears and prepares the way for the higher octave throat chakra stones to channel the truths that lay latent within the soul's realm. Once Blue Lace Agate has assisted in opening the throat chakra for the basic expression of thoughts and feelings, then Aquamarine, Indicolite, Celestite, and Gem Silica can be used to express higher wisdom through the power of the spoken word. When using these stones for this purpose, the Channeling Crystals (see *Crystal Healing*, Vol. II, pages 101-109) are also useful.

The throat chakra is a powerful energy center, one that has the capabilities of focussing and directing the sound current for the manifestation of creation. Blue Lace Agate, grounded, yet alive with peaceful presence, will enable individuals to access their own thoughts and feelings and bring them to life. Thus the foundation will be laid for greater fulfillment of the creative process.

CHAPTER XVI

CELESTITE

Celestite is imbued with the essence of the celestial realms. It is a clear, light blue, naturally terminated crystal which is usually found in cluster formation or in geodes. Celestite facilitates peaceful strength and mental clarity more than any of the other blue-ray stones. Even though it appears as if it were as hard as a heavenly blue quartz, it is actually very soft, fragile and sensitive to heat. If left in direct sunlight for very long, it is apt to fade to a lighter shade or even become colorless.

Have you ever gazed into a sky of blue and just allowed your mind to expand into the vastness of space? If so, then you already have a sense of the essence of Celestite. This beautiful crystalline entity has the potential to escort the human consciousness into the celestial realms, where thoughts can be freed from the cares and concerns of physical existence. The blue ray that Celestite reflects is a pure representation of the deep profound peace that is found when the mind transcends the lower levels of thought and establishes identification in pure being. Celestite assists one in maintaining a sense of personal security as the consciousness takes on greater dimension. It invites the mind to enter into a state of unlimited openness and total awareness, uninfluenced by thoughts, fragments of ideas, or conceptual notions. If placed at the Causal Chakra point, this light powder blue stone will elevate consciousness into a state of alert silence in which peaceful thought forms can be seeded into the causal levels of the mind.

Great power is embodied when peace of this kind is accessed. With total open awareness, undefined and devoid of expectation, a new type of strength comes into existence. In the past 'strength' has been generally defined in terms of 'might makes right. ' Human history has recorded many chapters where tribes, nations and countries have gained dominance merely through the strength invested in physical forces. Now, Celestite introduces a new definition of strength, one that transforms the nature of the battle sword into a field of flowers. The exquisite beauty of a flower is extremely simple and yet can provide a great lesson. A flower relies upon the innate trust that its seed will become rooted in the earth and knows that all of its needs will be provided for by the creator.

Celestite relays to us that same message of trust, showing us that our true security can be discovered if we but open our minds to the vast sea of spirit that is sure to see us through the trials and tribulations of earthly life. The vision that Celestite transmits, if placed upon the third eye, is one of peaceful co-existence and harmonious interaction with all other aspects of creation. Once this mental blueprint has been impressed upon the mind, it becomes a realistic possibility that can take tangible physical form.

Because sky blue is the color that is associated with the throat chakra, Celestite is also an effective crystal to wear or place at this energy center. It will help to translate the peaceful causal impressions into exact words that will further ground the reality of calm tranquility through the medium of verbal sound. Celestite is a wonderful stone to use in this way when consciously trying to ease tension in stressful circumstances or relationships. When used in this manner, it is helpful to also work with a Channeling Crystal to facilitate clear expression of Celestite's message (see *Crystal Healing*, Vol. II, pages 101-109). When meditated with, slept with, or carried, Celestite's ice blue frequency will serve to cool and tranquilize an over active mind, calm fiery emotions, and relax tense muscles as it transmits the true meaning of passivity. Its strong, loving, peaceful presence makes Celestite a reliable companion and a trustworthy friend in these transient times closing this century.

CHAPTER XVII

CHAROITE

Once again a stone comes to us representing the elegance of the purple ray. Like Luvulite (Sugulite-see *Crystal Enlightenment*, Vol. I, pages 121-125) Charoite has only recently been discovered in the remote Chara River region of Siberia. To date, this is the only known deposit. Like Luvulite, it too has manifested at a time when we, as a human race, are in dire need of its energy and essence. Working together with its purple ray comrades of Amethyst, Flourite and Luvulite, this newly arrived presence takes us yet a step closer to aligning with our souls, which the color purple represents.

Amethyst is the main meditation stone, to connect one with the innate wisdom at the third eye center (see *Crystal Enlightenment*, Vol. I, pages 78-82). Flourite is a multi-dimensional stone that organizes that inner wisdom to be perceived and used constructively by the mind (see *Crystal Enlightenment*, Vol. I, pages 106-113). Luvulite grounds the royal lavender essence from the ethereal into realms of thought to be used for mental comprehension, understanding and physical healing. Now, allow me to introduce Charoite who has remarkably appeared to perform another vitally important role in the manifestation of 'heaven on earth. '

Charoite is a picture stone which means that within its varied matrix of black, white, and numerous shades of purple, can be witnessed shapes, figures and semblances of conscious or subconscious meaning. Charoite often resembles the etheric realms as shapes of form and wisps of energy dance within its layered depths.

In the process of aligning with the soul, there are often conscious or subconscious fears that prevent us from totally embracing all that we truly are. All too often we are plagued by deep feelings of unworthiness, impossibility, guilt and fear. The social, religious and planetary conditioning that we have all been subjected to since birth often reinforces the idea that we are born in sin and therefore can never be unified with the creator while alive. To a greater or lesser degree, we have all been affected by these limited notions of reality. If we accept these mental programs and buy into that mind-set, the most we could ever hope for is communion with the Godhead once we are dead, and then only if we live and adhere to a very strict set of rules and dogmas. Charoite has come to share with us that there are other possibilities. In so doing, it will work its magic to help us clear the mental programs, attitudes, and constricting thought forms that keep our consciousness bound in sin, guilt and fear.

The fact that Charoite has the color black within its matrix indicates two important things. First, it means that this soul stone has the ability to ground the essence of the purple ray into the denser frequencies of thought and matter. It is there where the effects of restricted conditioning eventually manifest into mental and physical dis-ease. Secondly, Charoite has the power to dissolve the patterns of fear that create darkness in the mind and shadow the soul's light.

The first barrier that must be dissolved is the 'fear of fear' itself. Charoite has the ability to enter into the lower astral realms. It is there where fear prevents us from dealing with the root sources of mistrust that have been genetically inherited from generations of improper programming and limited thinking. Charoite encourages us to cross that initial threshold as it relays strength and courage into our minds.

The true battle that must be waged within each of us is that of confronting our own fear. We have all been controlled and weakened by the demon of fear who usurps our power and renders us useless to direct our own destinies. Charoite is fearless in the face of that demon and will lighten and brighten the darkest grimace on its face as it diffuses the beast with the light of the soul.

Fear can be very subtle in its ways. You may not even know that you are under its control. You may think, "Fear? No not me!" If so, it is necessary to look within and discern if you are in a state of perfect peace. Are you manifesting your full potential as a human-light being? Are you living in a state of harmony, love and joy in all aspects of your life? Are you perfectly healthy in your spiritual, mental, emotional and physical bodies? If not, then emotions such as fear, have more than likely been invisibly interwoven into your thoughts and feelings and Charoite can be of service in your life.

Be aware that if there are known or unknown fears lurking, Charoite will bring them to the surface. In this way Charoite is like Malachite or Black Obsidian in that you need to be fully aware of its effects before embarking upon personal experience with this stone. You may need to take time and effort after meditation with Charoite to process fears which will be uncovered and made obvious. If you are aware and prepared, great clearing and healing can occur.

Besides surfacing fears, Charoite also assists by empowering your thoughts with the courage and strength of will to dissolve the fear patterns existing within the mind. It is one of the most powerful stones to use when confronting demons of fear, whether they be aspects of yourself or external entities that have become attached to your aura. (For more information on this subject please read, *Crystal Healing*, Vol. II, pages 75-79). Once these patterns are released, the soul's true purpose can be fulfilled.

Charoite can be used at the third eye center in crystal healings when a person is ready to consciously let go of fear and become aware of his/her soul's purpose. When facilitating a crystal healing of this kind, first follow the therapeutic procedures detailed in *Crystal Healing*, Vol. II and assist the recipient to release the fear. Secondly, work with him/her to redefine who he/she is according to the soul's wisdom and discover what this life's true purpose actually is. Finally work out a strong maintenance plan that will bring into manifestation the soul's light through daily activities.

Charoite can also be used when releasing external entities in exorcisms. In these cases, again follow therapeutic procedures and be familiar with Chapter Five in *Crystal Healing*, Volume II. Place at least one piece of Charoite at the third eye and another over the area of the body where the entity has become attached. This part of the body (or chakra center) will probably be weakened or dis-eased. Assist the recipient to empower his/her own will and insist that the outside force be gone forever. If the entity is amenable, send it back to its source or into the light. If it is not, absolutely insist that it leave, surround it with light, and have the recipient affirm that it will never again reenter the aura. Continue to use Charoite over the third eye and area of attachment as you surround the body with clear quartz clusters to seal the aura. Assist the recipient to become aware of his/her soul purpose. It is important when using Charoite in this way that a strong maintenance plan be constructed so that the recipient can continue to strengthen the will, stabilize new mental patterns, and create a sense of personal independence and security. (See *Crystal Healing*, Vol. II, Chapter VI).

Charoite can be carried, worn, or meditated with whenever you want to align with the soul's essence and become aware of its true purpose upon the earth. It can be used to diminish fears of any kind, especially those that limit the expression of your innate light and its manifestation. Charoite is a wonderful companion to take to bed with you, along with Amethyst, when the sleep state is disturbed with lower astral battles or fears that will surface in dreams from the subconscious.

In short, Charoite is the soul stone that has dominion over fear. We, too, can have that same dominion. Then, and only then, will the soul force unite with the body, will the doors to our hearts swing wide open and will our minds be totally free. The courage exemplified in Charoite is now being transmitted, enabling us to align with the purple ray of the soul and fulfill our destinies upon this earth.

CHAPTER XVIII

CUPRITE

Like Hematite, Cuprite is given birth to when ethereal gases work their magic on earthly metals. Hematite is created when iron is exposed to oxygen and Cuprite is born when copper is exposed to oxygen. Being the crystal of copper, Cuprite is commonly known as 'Ruby Copper' and is surpassed by none for its true blood-red color. Even the reddest of Carnelian cannot compare in depth and degree to high grade Cuprite.

Keeping pace with its cohort Hematite, Cuprite ranks among the top three stones that have the ability to directly affect the blood stream. With Carnelian's purification abilities and Hematite's blood strengthening properties, we have the means at hand to work directly with the cleansing, healing, and maintenance of the vital fluid in the physical body. Now, let's include Cuprite in our repertoire of powerful red-energy blood stones.

Oxygen is absolutely essential for our physical survival. It is through the breath that we receive the oxygen that feeds all of the organs, tissues and cells of the physical body. It is also through the breath that we assimilate what the Yogi's of the East refer to as 'prana, ' or vital life force. If the physical body is not nourished with food it is still capable of surviving for weeks. We can also live for days without water. But without oxygen and prana we cannot maintain physical existence for even ten minutes. Many therapies have been developed which focus on revitalizing the physical, mental, and emotional bodies by using the power of the breath. The more oxygen and prana that is assimilated into the human system through the bloodstream, the more hope there is for physical healing, reenergization, increased vitality, and inspiration.

Prana is the all pervasive spirit force which has a direct effect upon the subtle bodies and oxygen is the means through which that force is directed into the physical body. Therefore, oxygenating the blood and charging the body with the pranic life force are two main keys to heal and rebuild the human structure. Cuprite gracefully, yet powerfully, embraces both the subtle and the physical, blending the vital life force with matter in a brilliant embodiment of true red energy. When placed or worn on the physical body, Cuprite's vibrant color is reflected into the aura. It actually invites greater pranic forces into the individual's energy field to be utilized by the breath and transferred into the cells of the body.

Since Cuprite is given birth to when a red metal (copper) is exposed to oxygen it acts as a catalyst through which greater oxygenation can occur in the physical body. Cuprite can be placed on the body directly over areas that are dis-eased, sluggish or in need of a boost of energy. Used in conjunction with breathing exercises and increased aerobic movement, Cuprite can be worn or meditated with to improve overall vitality and well being. It is a perfect stone to use over the chest area to rebuild lung tissue after inhaling polluted atmospheres or smoking cigarettes. Cuprite is also one of the most effective stones to use when working with AIDS or cancer patients. It will usher in greater life force to rebuild the circulatory and immune systems by increasing the prana and oxygen in the red and white blood cells (see AIDS Chapter, pages 261-266).

Copper is known to be one of the best conductors of energy. Legend has it that in the ancient days of Egypt the great pyramids had capstones that were made of copper and crystal. These capstones were specifically designed to conduct high frequency energies to be used in teleportation and telepathic communication with other star systems. Copper is very soft and maleable and is ruled by Venus, the planet of love. Cuprite inherited the same attributes as its parent planet and is capable of adjusting itself to lovingly conduct life force frequencies into the human system. If placed directly over the heart, arteries and/or veins it will serve to transmit vital currents of energy into and through the circulatory system.

Cuprite often unites with Chrysocolla (see *Crystal Enlightenment*, Vol. I, pages 101-102, 147-148) which is a feminine power stone. This marriage between vital red and soothing blue provides us with yet more insight into the multi-purpose uses of this stone. Chrysocolla adds a softening element to the intense red energy that Cuprite alone projects. Balancing opposite ends of the spectrum, this combination of color rays can be used for the rejuvenation of women's reproductive organs when placed over the uterus and ovary areas. It is a wonderful companion for women who are going through the change of life, are recovering from childbirth, cesarean sections, hysterectomies or who are suffering from infertility or menstrual disorders.

Cuprite-Chrysocolla is also a great friend to men (or women) who are consciously trying to soften over-aggressive tendencies with greater feeling from the heart. Chrysocolla exemplifies feminine power and Cuprite represents masculine assertion. The marriage between the two shows us that it is possible to harmonize our own male and female sides as it demonstrates balanced partnerships. Besides blending its energies with Chrysocolla, Cuprite can also be occasionally united with the indigo blue of Azurite and the deep green of Malachite.

Being such a powerful red presence Cuprite has gained the nickname of 'The Warrior Stone. ' Like Rhodonite and some forms of Larimar, Cuprite will assist in strengthening the will so that more personal responsibility can be accepted for the creations of one's life. In so doing, greater potential is achieved and personal growth and freedom are attained. It is a stone that when meditated with, empowers one to make the necessary changes in attitude, feeling and life-style in order to promote a fuller sense of wholeness and wellness. With the empowerment of the will, it becomes possible to replace deadly feelings and attitudes such as guilt and worthlessness with self-forgiveness and self-love.

Cuprite is a particularly good partner for people who have been diagnosed as 'terminal' and are determined to heal themselves and radically change their lives and views. Cuprite is a stone that empowers all aspects of the being with greater vitality while rebuilding the structures (either subtle or physical) that have deteriorated due to improper systems of living. Great strength, creative energy, regenerative properties and courage are embodied by this stone which can easily and effectively be transmitted to an open mind, heart and body.

Cuprite is mined in the four-corner's region of the United States, which is one of the opening power vortexes in the Southwest. It is usually opaque and is recognized by its true deep red color. Cuprite is not as common as some of the other healing stones but is becoming more available to those who are truly in need of its transmission. It is a valuable addition for crystal healers who are working with cancer and AIDS patients as well as for those who are making conscious decisions about who they choose to be, where they are going, and how to rebuild and recreate their lives.

CHAPTER XIX

DIOPTASE

As clear as deep green waters and as powerful as emeralds, Dioptase comes to us as a beacon of hope for healing the inner realms of the heart chakra. For deep seeded forgotten heartaches and ancient wounds festering in forgotten chambers of feeling, Dioptase is unsurpassed in its ability to transmit a potent deep green ray into the inner recesses of the heart. Dioptase has the potential to send its dynamic healing energy into any aspect of the heart that has been emotionally wounded in relationships with others.

We are already aware of the soothing qualities of Green Aventurine and the dynamic strength of Green Tourmaline as heart healers. Now let's give ample attention to another exceptional crystalline structure. Dioptase is imbued with the power to heal and renurture those parts of the self that have been emotionally abandoned while experiencing life's inevitable heartbreaks. When placed at the center of the chest, Dioptase will courageously cross the threshold of the heart's natural protective shield and dissolve the defenses that serve to inhibit vulnerability. Once Dioptase has entered into the inner sanctums, where suffering has been conveniently suppressed, it will send its healing rays into forgotten feelings of betrayal, abandonment, grief, and sorrow. Then, its healing green energy will activate the heart's natural ability to heal and reap the harvest from love's lessons. Used in conjunction with the Isis Crystal (see pages 153-171) Dioptase will lend great comfort and contentment to hearts that through loss, fear to love again. Used at the third eye point, Dioptase will bring insight and understanding to those whose guilt and false sense of responsibility have taken on the burden of trying to control the destinies of others.

Dioptase will renew love's power to heal any wound, however deep or scarred. It will rejuvenate the heart's courage to love even more deeply, with more commitment and dedication than ever before. The unique energy that Dioptase emits has the power to connect one to the heart of hearts, the source of love itself. The pure essence of love that can be experienced and embraced on that level will heal emotional injuries and open the way to transmute emotional pain and resurrect the Christ presence within. It will transmit the power of love itself, assisting in the identification with internal peace and compassion, instead of with transitory realities, people or situations.

The pain of love that is experienced at the loss of relationships is deeply rooted in the unconscious sense of separation with one's self. Longing for reunion with our own souls, we search for it on the outside of us in the form of relationships. But, no matter how much love we receive from external sources, it can never really fulfill the sense of emptiness from within. Dioptase is the most powerful crystalline entity that can heal the wounds of lost loves so that the heart can find its true fulfillment within the self.

Dioptase

Dioptase will first clear away the old perceptions in the way that we relate to love. Then its vital deep powerful green essence will help to rebuild a new foundation, the cornerstone of which rests in the essence of the most powerful force in the universe, that of compassion. Through continued use and meditation with Dioptase, one can refocus his/her identity into the very heart of God and learn the true meaning of unconditional love. Used with Pink Calcite, Dioptase will assist one to exist in a state of being that will translate a new meaning of love into every relationship and circumstance, and into every thought, feeling and action.

We are very fortunate to receive the blessings of this incredibly beautiful stone. Aren't we ready to give up the old definition and ways of love that can only result in loss and pain? Isn't it time to heal the regions of the heart that have been bruised and battered through trying to experience love in such a limited way? Aren't we ready to sink into the core of our beings and BECOME that which we have sought after for lifetimes? The time is now and Dioptase is here to serve in the transmutation of emotional pain and the transformation of our beings.

Dioptase is often confused with Emerald crystals as it offers the same verdant gem quality columnar crystals. The color ranges from deep green to bluish-green and is breathtaking to behold. Dioptase is expensive and fairly difficult to locate, being mined mostly in Russia and South-West Africa. I highly suggest that you put the beam out for it and pay the price. I promise you won't be sorry.

CHAPTER XX
LARIMAR

Larimar is a stone that relays the peaceful emanations from the Deva of the Blue Ray. It is mined on an island in the Caribbean Sea. Much like Luvulite, this stone is currently only found in one vicinity and serves a very unique purpose for humanity at this time. Having its origin near the beautiful blue Caribbean, this stone has captured the essence of both water and air. Water relates to the emotions and air to the thoughts. Therefore, Larimar has a very specialized relationship for both the emotions of the heart and the thoughts of the mind. It is as if this stone creates a needed and necessary synapse between thought and feeling, establishing a connection of peace that will unite the mind and the heart with the blue ray of tranquility.

Negative thoughts often produce turbulent feelings. In the same way, unbalanced emotions can cloud the mind's perception. Larimar is like an angelic thread that weaves the impressions of peaceful harmony between the heart and the mind. It also helps to neutralize and dissolve old conflicting patterns that can keep one separate and disassociated from certain aspects of the self. Placed at the heart and third eye, in conjunction with Lepidolite in crystal healing layouts, noticeable progress can be made with schizophrenic disorders or any physical malady that would result from the mind being out of alignment with the heart.

Larimar is volcanic in nature and has evolved from a hot fiery source, yet it is the coolest, softest blue imaginable. From this stone we can learn how to cool down the fire energy within ourselves and how to calm burning emotions such as anger, frustration, lust, and greed. Larimar is unsurpassed in its ability to cool the hot fires of anger that can burn within the solar plexus. Used over the solar plexus, liver, and stomach areas in meditation or in crystal healings, Larimar works wonders in transmuting raging rivers of red anger into blue reservoirs of personal peace. This is one of the blessings offered by the Blue Deva residing within Larimar.

Larimar can be placed on any area of the body where there is excess energy as it will cool and redistribute the life force to deficient areas. To do this, one stone should be placed on top of the area of excess. Another stone should be placed in the area where the energy is to be redirected. Then use a single quartz generator to relocate the energy by moving it towards the desired location. Larimar is also a good stone to be used by acupuncturists for balancing the life force in the meridians of the body. Or, it is easily used by lay persons who wish to reestablish balanced energy currents between their own chakras.

Besides white cloud-like reticulations, Larimar will also occasionally display green or red dendritic patterns against the soft blue. These stones are particularly good for people who are soft, gentle and non-assertive and therefore tend to get walked on and pushed around. The red-green Larimar will build personal projective powers for these gentle souls who need to learn how to say "No, you may not abuse or take advantage of me. " This ability to say "NO" will increase personal strength and assist these peace lovers to maintain their softness while balancing their overly passive nature with deliberate assertive action. These stones are particularly good for children as they enter the school system where bullies abound. Used with Rhodonite, red Larimar strengthens the peace and love within children. Simultaneously, it will assist in developing the fortitude to assert those spiritual powers outward into their world.

The scenes embodied in Larimar resemble an attuned artist's rendition of the combined elements of sea and sky. It depicts beautiful soft blue landscapes, blending the motion of the ocean with the gentle wisps of clouds. The ocean, as well as clouds, are always in a state of perpetual motion and change, never maintaining a sense of permanence. This transient beauty has always captured and inspired the souls of artists, musicians, and writers. Larimar can be used by such talented persons to stimulate creativity, activate the imagination, and inspire the spirit.

Larimar is also a powerful healing stone that can be meditated with, carried, or worn when troubled by a sense of physical impermanence or disturbed by the transitory nature of life. It can be a calming and tranquil friend for teenagers. During this particular phase of life, young adults often become depressed and discouraged as they try to establish their identity in the world while facing the realization that nothing on the physical plane will last forever. This indeed is one of the spiritual initiations along the path toward enlightenment. It actually acts as a catalyst in the quest for greater truth and meaning in life. Larimar is an excellent stone to use in trying times such as these. It expresses the ever changing nature of life while simultaneously relaying the sense of eternal peace into the heart of the matter.

The Crystalline Transmission

Being etheric in nature, this peace stone transmits pure spiritual substance into the higher chakras in the head. In so doing, it can be used in the creation of new thought forms. Used in crystal healings at the third eye, hairline, crown center, or causal chakra point, Larimar assists in creating new etheric synapses between the Soul Star, the mind, and the physical body. As these fresh lines of energy are stabilized, the mind will be capable of functioning on higher brain wave frequencies, enabling new circuits to link thoughts with spirit. This will allow one to be in an active state of thinking while simultaneously maintaining a conscious connection to the peaceful quiet of deep meditation. A perfect companion for Larimar, when used for this purpose, is Gem Silica (see *Crystal Enlightenment*, Vol. I, pages 101-105). When placed together at the third eye, Gem Silica will open up the etheric vision so that Larimar can channel and ground the etheric substance into the mind for the intuition and the intellect to utilize. Since sky blue is the natural color for the throat chakra, Larimar also can be placed there when one desires to verbally express the newly formulated ideas. Larimar can also be worn or placed at the throat chakra to soothe the burning pain of sore throats and tonsillitis.

As you can see, Larimar is like Gem Silica, in that it is a multi-purpose stone, and can be used in many ways, for many circumstances, by many people. The angelic presence that resides within Larimar is unconditional in its love and acceptance of everyone. Thus, all who choose to use Larimar will be benefited by its peaceful emanations. Use this stone when you want to awaken this celestial peace within yourself, or use it in a crystal healing with another person to facilitate calmness. Call upon the Deva of the Blue Ray and evoke her powers into your life. Know that as you identify with this Deva, you become it, and you inherit the quality of tranquility in an ever changing world.

CHAPTER XXI

LEPIDOLITE

Lepidolite is much like Kunzite in that it manifests the pink-purple ray. Whenever this new color ray presents itself, it can be assumed that we will be working with an energy that will assist in balancing the heart (pink) with the mind (purple). Lepidolite will vary in color range from soft pale pink to deep dark purple, but most often the two hues are gracefully combined into a perfect blending of each. If however, the Lepidolite stone has a greater degree of pink, it will work more effectively to soothe a troubled heart. If there is more of the purple ray, that stone will be more useful to calm and balance an overactive mind.

There is a growing need these days to balance polarities, whether they be the male and female sides of ourselves, the physical and the spiritual, or the heart and the mind. The acknowledgment and acceptance of each aspect is essential if we are to come to peaceful terms with ourselves and create a sense of personal wholeness. Lepidolite is arriving on the scene in these times of mergence as a messenger of the androgynous way and to assist us in answering such questions as: How do we build the bridge between the soul feelings of the heart and the conscious impressions of the higher mind? How do we create a new way of being by blending the knowing of the mind with the knowing of the heart? How can we acknowledge and credit two seemingly opposing aspects of ourselves into unification in a way that will ultimately give more credence and power to each part? Lepidolite, in its ability to perfectly harmonize the pink-purple ray, is an ideal teacher of these lessons. It is an example of how to build the bridge that facilitates the wedding of heart and mind.

Besides Lepidolite's ability to unify the mind and the heart, it is also a powerful healer of whatever may be inhibiting this mergence. Too often people are overidentified with either their thinking processes and thought forms (generally male) or their emotional programs and reactions (generally female). Lepidolite blends the soft pink of Rose Quartz with the gentle purple of Amethyst and will take the energy within for calming and self-healing. As its influence sinks into the inner realms, the patterns of overidentification with mental or emotional programs are softened. This is a stone that can be used in crystal healing layouts anywhere between the upper forehead and the solar plexus. It has a very calming and soothing effect whether it is placed near the heart chakra to reawaken 'spiritual feeling' or on the third eye to rekindle intuitive knowing.

The material found in Lepidolite is lithium mica. Lithium is a soft silver-white metal and is the lightest solid element. Salts from lithium are widely used in the treatment of schizophrenia and manic-depression. So much of the schizophrenic tendency revolves around the separate personalities that develop in an individual when the feelings are out of alignment with the thoughts. Isn't it interesting that a drug is made from a stone which in its natural form would be used to balance the mind and the heart? Lepidolite can be worn, taken in gem remedies (see *Crystal Enlightenment*, Vol. I, pages 18-19), placed in bath water, meditated with, or placed upon the body to soothe, balance, and harmonize the mental and emotional bodies.

In some Lepidolite we have an extra added attraction! Pink Tourmaline often finds its way into this stone. What better companion to have along with a balanced heart and mind than one that will better enable the joyous expression of love? Once again, isn't is interesting that the mergence of these two stones would serve such a common purpose? Once the Lepidolite serves its internalized purpose of building a common bridge to accommodate both the heart and the mind, Pink Tourmaline will express the dynamic power of love outward into the world. These stones are particularly useful for people who are introverted, shy, or unable to express love in an externalized way. The exuberance of Pink Tourmaline, intimately bonded with the soft gentle nature of Lepidolite, enables greater transmission of unified thought and feeling through the heart chakra. Thank you Lepidolite and Pink Tourmaline for merging in a way that so efficiently serves our human purpose.

CHAPTER XXII
MOLDAVITE TEKTITE

Tektites are generally defined as silica based glassy meteorites. Most tektites have scarred surfaces, are tar black to blackish brown in color and are rarely larger than two inches wide. Moldavite belongs to the tektite family and is one of the rarest varieties manifesting in a gem quality bottle green to brown green color.

There are two theories concerning the origin of Moldavite Tektite. One is that it has evolved in the deep archives of outer space and is a true meteorite. The other school of thought, which is more widely accepted, is that Moldavite Tektite was formed from rock which melted after being hit by a meteorite. This would indicate that Moldavite Tektite is a rare and wonderful mergence of that which is extraterrestrial in origin with that which is born out of the womb of the earth. Whatever the case may be, these advanced crystalline structures entered the earth's atmosphere in meteorite, asteroid or comet form to serve a very special purpose for those inhabiting the earth at this time. Being known as 'the extra-terrestrial gemstone, ' Moldavite Tektite is among the rarest of gems and is obviously a true gift from the heavens. Manifesting an unearthly green ray, Moldavite Tektite will lend its extraterrestrial transmission to profoundly impact the consciousness of those who choose to attune to its frequency.

Moldavite Tektite essentially has two important functions. First, it is one of the only stones in existence on the planet at this time that will assist Star Children to acclimate to an earth plane environment. Moldavite Tektite has very much in common with beings originating from the Pleiades, Sirius, Orion and other star systems. It, too, has travelled a long distance, through vast oceans of space, to arrive on this planet named "Terra. " It, too, has its origin in regions and realms that until recently were beyond our comprehension. It, too, is intimately connected to sources of knowledge and energy that will serve in the healing and awakening of the human race. Sharing these vital similarities, Moldavite Tektite will lend an ear of understanding and a heart of compassion to those beings who are struggling to adjust in a world of such drastically opposing polarities. The new green ray that Moldavite transmits is a combination of green and brown, of healing (green) on the earth (brown).

Many souls now inhabiting physical bodies have come into this world seemingly unequipped to deal with the elements of human suffering, emotionalism and the material realities inherent on this plane of existence. The source that these highly sensitive beings originated from was very different in nature and spiritual climate than that of this earth. Our earth, named Terra, is indeed a very powerful, moody and beautiful creature, which can never be underestimated or accurately predicted. Her peoples are as diversified as is her terrain. Her fertility and ability to yield life is unsurpassed in our universe. And yet, she is temperamental and can become angry and suddenly reactive. Now, Terra has become fearful for her own survival and has sent out a call into the mighty universe for assistance in her own liberation from the life forms upon her surface that would seek to do her harm.

This call has been heard from afar. Now, besides the chosen ones (see 'those who choose to stay, ' *Crystal Healing*, Vol. II, pages 157-159) who have worked diligently on Terra's behalf for millenniums, other soular breeds are incarnating in order to reseed the earth with a new race of being. The only problem is that for many of these freshly incarnating souls this is their first time in a physical body. Many of them haven't a clue as to how to deal with inhaling and exhaling an atmosphere, let alone dealing with such things as the physical senses, emotions, and mind sets such as separateness and sin. Many of these star souls are unable to fully integrate their expanded consciousness into the physical brain structure and are experiencing epilepsy, brain imbalances and malfunctions, and autism. Moldavite Tektite can be placed on any (or all) of the chakras on the head to treat any of the above mentioned dis-eases. It can also be successfully used in the treatment of the psychological-emotional distresses that can accompany such maladjusted human-light beings. The healing earth-green of Moldavite Tektite greatly assists, not only in activating the healing energy so vitally needed for these souls, but also in the grounding process and evolutionary advancement of these new breeds upon the earth.

The second purpose that Moldavite Tektite will serve is in conscious communication with the star-seed sources of origin. It is a healing balm for the deep longing of so many people (the chosen ones) to 'go home. ' This heartache is a common malady among those who are consciously remembering who they are and where they came from. If placed upon the third eye, Moldavite will assist in conscious communication with the source related to as 'home. ' It also relays into the mind of those using this stone the message that "transforming Terra is of utmost importance and the earth has become the chosen home. " This may come as a severe shock to many souls who are waiting for the big opportunity to beam-up; but harsh as it may seem, the message remains the same.

Once star souls enter the earth plane experience and master the five senses, they undergo an extraordinary evolutionary process which is unknown and incomprehensible to those folks 'back home. ' They have engaged in experiences and have grown in ways that have transformed the very nature of their beings and altered their identity forever. Returning to the star system related to as 'home' would be like moving back to your parents' house after you have been out in the world on your own for forty years and expecting everything to be the same as when you left.

Those beings who are freshly arriving, as well as those who have been through the entire physical plane cycle, are now at a bountiful harvest time. They have an incredible and unique opportunity at hand to literally recreate the earth in a way that will encompass the spiritual laws of 'home' into this physical world. That is the purpose. That is why these souls are here. That is the hope and the glory of this whole divine experiment. Moldavite Tektite will ease the deep longing for 'home' and assist in creating the willingness to be here and stay grounded in order to create a reality that includes so much more than the one known in a far distant past. It will assist star souls to accept with pleasure the opportunities that exist now on Terra for full scale transformation.

Moldavite Tektite, if placed or worn at the heart chakra, will heal the longing for 'home' so that home will truly be where the heart is. If placed at the third eye and/or meditated with, it will transmit and translate original laws and revolutionary new ideas into the consciousness for manifestation onto the earth. If used consistently, it will activate the higher brain centers and reawaken latent memories, knowledge, and information. Moldavite Tektite can also facilitate direct telepathic communication with extraterrestrials or friends 'back home. ' In so doing, evolutionary information can be communicated back and forth. This will benefit both those on the earth and those beings aligned with the same star system yet not incarnated in the physical plane at this time. To increase the effects of this type of interdimensional communication, use Moldavite Tektite in conjunction with The Transmitter Crystals (see *Crystal Healing*, Vol. II, pages 111-119).

As with Selenite, it is important when working with Moldavite Tektite to work with other stones that will assist in grounding and assimilating the energies that will be conducted through this higher octave crystalline form. Black Tourmaline, Hematite, Smoky Quartz, Black Onyx, dark Rhodonite and Hawkeye are all beneficial stones to use when working with Moldavite Tektite. They will facilitate the proper integration of the stellar rays that Moldavite transmits. If not properly grounded, Moldavite Tektite can take you 'too far out there' and leave you spaced out and disassociated with the physical plane, which in return can create even more turmoil. Use this stone with those that need to accept physical reality and balance with the earth plane elements. Please do not use this powerful energy to merely identify with the ethers. Instead, use it to incorporate the reality of other worlds onto Terra. Moldavite Tektite answered the call that Terra sent out for healing. It is here to transmit its earth-green ray into the very heart and soul of Terra's star breeds.

CHAPTER XXIII

RHODONITE

Rhodonite is an opaque pink stone with either dark black or white inclusions in it. If the inclusions are dark (manganese oxide) the pink color in the stone tends to be dark as well. If the inclusions are light (fowlerite), the stone will generally also be a lighter shade of pink. Rhodonite is similar in color to Rhodochrosite, yet pinker, with dendritic markings. Occasionally it forms in terminated crystals, however it is usually found cut into cabochons or tumbled.

Rhodonite is an important heart chakra stone in that it will assist to usher the love force onto the physical plane. Being opaque, Rhodonite will ground the pink love ray, whereas transparent heart stones such as Pink Calcite or Kunzite will activate the love energy. In the process of healing, Rose Quartz and Pink Smithsonite can be used to nurture the inner realms of the heart. Then soft, pink, striated Kunzite will activate the love and prepare it for external expression. Having the way opened, it is then possible for Pink Tour-

247

maline and Rhodonite to enter into activity as that love is given birth to in the physical world. Pink Tourmaline will dynamically transmit the heart's joy into expression. The grounding frequency of Rhodonite will allow the love to enter into various mundane activities, such as brushing your teeth, doing the dishes, grocery shopping, or driving to work.

Rhodonite is the most beneficial stone to wear or carry in your pocket when you want to maintain a loving state while in the midst of every day life. If you want the support of a sturdy, solid friend when you ask for a raise, contend with relationship disturbances, or need to feel strong, yet loving, take Rhodonite along. It will assist you to stay in your heart while holding your ground. This is especially good for women who tend to feel that to love is to give in, so that peace can be maintained. Yet in doing so, personal integrity is often sacrificed and the most appropriate action is seldom taken. Rhodonite is a great stone to meditate with when restructuring disciplinary methods with children or resolving compliancy patterns with partners. When you want to take your stand, maintain your love, and channel the strength of your heart into action, use Rhodonite.

Rhodonite is a wonderful stone to use in crystal healing layouts. Used at the heart chakra and solar plexus it will help to replace erratic emotions with a secure sense of feeling loved. When placed upon the groin points or at the center of the pubic bone, Rhodonite serves as a powerful initiator of the love force into the roots of physical plane reality, especially if the stone has black inclusions. It can also be placed anywhere on the body, over physically dis-eased internal organs or tissues, to relay the love vibration into the cells. This is particularly effective if the breath is focussed into the specific locality and visualization methods connect the consciousness into the area.

Many things can be healed if given enough love. Rhodonite makes the powerful statement that love can be an inseparable part of earthly action and will prove it if worked with consistently. It will transmit the strength of the heart and the power of love into all facets of everyday life. Learn from Rhodonite and then embody the power. So be it!

CHAPTER XXIV

SMITHSONITE

Smithsonite has an exceptionally soft, gentle nature. In its natural state it looks like layers of silky bubbles. Smithsonite ranges in color from pastel blue, to light green, to soft pink. It is unique in its ability to tranquilize the senses with its restoring pearly luster.

This stone, with its soft nurturing presence, serves in much the same way as Rose Quartz in that it soothes, comforts and tends to heal the tough blows that life can offer. Generally speaking, Smithsonite will usher its delicate essence into the inner sanctums of the self to nurture the child within. Insecure adult behavior patterns are often rooted in traumatic childhood experiences, such as feeling unloved, unaccepted or unnurtured. Smithsonite will penetrate into the heart of the matter to automatically lend a calm healing presence. At times its effect is so deep and subtle that you may be unaware that it has had an effect at all. But, then you notice that you feel better, like someone just left you flowers or tidied up your internal environment. When working with Smithsonite on such deep inner levels, it may also be necessary to use such stones as Gem Silica or Azurite on the third eye and Malachite at the solar plexus (see *Crystal Healing*, Vol. II, pages 34-37, 46-48). These stones will help to bring into conscious awareness that which is being released and healed.

Smithsonite's softening energy is like loosening the tight stretch of an elastic band that is about ready to snap. It replaces the strain with graceful suppleness of movement. Therefore, this stone is excellent to use in situations where stress has accumulated to the breaking point. Smithsonite is the perfect stone to wear or carry in high anxiety situations or life-styles to ease the tension that can eventually wear down the nervous system, create heart pressure and take the joy out of living. Smithsonite can be used in crystal healing layouts after nervous, emotional, or mental breakdowns. Its softness will assist to neutralize the effects of over extended and over assertive states of being. Smithsonite can be used in conjunction with massage therapy, to ease muscle tension and strain due to anxiety related psychological-emotional problems. It can be placed at any of the chakra centers or directly on top of the spine during and/or after massages. It will ease muscle tension and reconstruct new lines of energy which will be better able to channel tranquil vibrations into the nervous system.

Smithsonite is an excellent stone to have present at births and makes a wonderful companion to mothers in labor as it directs its mellow magic into the childbirth process. No midwife should be without this stone. It is extremely helpful to have the mother hold onto a blue-green colored Smithsonite during the transition and pushing phases in order to soften and soothe the intensity of giving birth. Afterwards, Smithsonite continues to provide comfort to the freshly arrived infant as it maintains a gentle, warm, secure frequency for the child to bathe in. Used in remedies or placed on or near newly arrived souls, this stone will prove itself to be a valuable friend in helping babies gently adjust to the material plane realities of sleeping, eating, digesting and relating to the physical world.

The most common color that Smithsonite will reflect is a pastel blue-green ray, vibrating the peacefulness of blue and the healing essence of green. Similar in color and energy to high grade Chrysocolla and Gem Silica, this ray of Smithsonite is very much related to water and the calming of emotions. It serves in much the same way as the quieting effect of ocean waves, a pure mountain stream, or a deep clear lake. Placing this stone at the third eye will assist one to mentally visualize these watery sanctuaries and in so doing, deepen meditation. Blue-green Smithsonite can also be used to bring into balance the red related emotions of anger, resentment, jealousy and anxiety.

Smithsonite also manifests in a soft pink ray which of course will pertain to healing the heart. Placed on the chest in crystal healing layouts, pink Smithsonite will work much like Rose Quartz in the internalization of the love force. But, where Rose Quartz will assist the individual to love oneself, Pink Smithsonite will aid one to feel loved by the external world. It will help one to feel nurtured by the forces of the universe, the angels, people, and the elements of the earth. Pink Smithsonite can sink as deep as Rose Quartz into the inner sanctums of the heart but it also serves in the externalized expression of love.

Pink Smithsonite is a perfect stone for children (or adult-children) who have been abandoned and/or abused. Because of experiences such as these, the primal security base has often been shattered. If worn, held, slept with, carried, placed upon at the heart chakra, or meditated with, this magical love stone will help to rebuild the sense of safety and peace within as well as with life itself.

The Crystalline Transmission

Smithsonite is a stone that can be placed over any part of the body to directly relay a sense of calm well-being. Its presence will transmit peaceful impressions not only to the mental and emotional bodies, but into the tissues and organs of the physical body as well. In so doing, the entirety of the individual feels loved, taken care of, nurtured and comforted. Add this one to your collection. You won't be sorry!

CHAPTER XXV
SUNSTONE AND STARSTONE

Sunstone is a sparkling orange or red-brown stone that reflects a red metallic glitter. Starstone mirrors a clear-blue luminescence against a black background, resembling a star-filled sky on a crystal clear night. The bright spangled reflections that Sunstone and Starstone are known for are actually caused by light dancing on tiny flecks of Hematite. Knowing that Hematite is the Predominate Power Stone that most effectively ushers the spirit force into the physical reality, we can conclude that Hematite's presence has worked its magic on these two stones. Both Sunstone and Starstone have been through the process of blending earth and heaven and are endowed with wondrous alchemical powers.

True Sunstone and Starstone are rare, hard to find and expensive. But, both of these stones also have man-made representatives which resemble the essence and nature of the original stones. 'Goldstone' and 'Black Goldstone' are the names for the artificial counterparts of these magical crystalline entities. They are the only two man-made stones that I have ever been guided to use in crystal healings. Of course, if you can locate and afford the natural stones, by all means use them. If not, Goldstone and Black Goldstone will serve in the place of Sunstone and Starstone with similar effects.

Sunstone and Starstone are polarity stones likened to the brightness of the sun in the middle of the day and the radiance of the stars in the depth of the night. Each serves its own individual, as well as common purpose, as it works its magic in ways that no other stone can do.

Sunstone ushers the illustrious essence of the sun into any area where it is placed. It is common knowledge that without the light of our sun there would be no life upon the earth. For that reason the sun was the main object of focus and worship in most ancient religions and ways of life. Today, it is as if we have forgotten how vital the sun is to our survival. Not only is it the very light of our lives, it is also the star through which we can gain access to the higher dimensions (see Sun Meditations, pages 46-49). Sunstone is a perfect stone to use when practicing the Sun Meditations. It can be taped to the third eye area or held in the outstretched hands.

Sunstone is also a powerful partner to assist in connecting with the internal source of light when practicing other forms of meditation. Sunstone is a wonderful companion to carry or wear when desiring to maintain a conscious connection to the light while participating in the activities of daily life. In crystal healings, Sunstone can be placed anywhere on the body where you want to activate greater light force and draw upon the regenerative powers of the sun. It is especially helpful at the solar plexus area to lighten the weight of suppressed or heavy emotions. Being alchemical in nature, Sunstone will assist in transmuting and transforming anything which is not working in harmony with the laws of light.

Sunstone and Starstone

Starstone is the other side of the sun, that which exists when the sun sinks below the horizon and is out of view. When working with the laws of polarity that exist upon this planet, it is necessary to understand that the light exists even when we cannot see it. It is indeed helpful to acknowledge the natural cycle of the sun, and to know that it will rise again. In the same way, it is very comforting to be aware that spiritual guidance is available every step along the way, even when in the midst of personal darkness or involved in learning lessons that seem beyond comprehension. Starstone is for those times. When meditated with, worn, carried or placed on the body in crystal healings, Starstone will transmute the deepest despair into the faith and the knowing that everything is truly in divine right order.

When placed at the third eye, Starstone will help you through the 'darkest hour of the night. ' It will transmit the understanding that when the night is the darkest, the stars are the brightest and you are not left without light, even for one moment. Starstone, with its dark brilliance, assists in dissolving the illusion that there is anything but light, even when it cannot be seen. What a blessing it is to have a tool and a teacher such as Starstone. It is a reminder that all is perfect, even when consumed in the depth of human struggle. Starstone will show the light in times when it cannot be seen or felt.

Starstone is an ideal stone to use in crystal healings along with Hematite at the first chakra points to ground the stellar rays into the body. Being alchemical in nature, Starstone will initiate the wonders of metamorphosis in order to transform the nature of existence here on earth. It can be used over any part of the body that is in need of grounding, while it adds a little extra ingredient of magic. Used at the third eye in crystal healings, Starstone can also assist one to make conscious connection and establish communication with other star systems or beings not of this earth.

Sunstone and Starstone, or their man-made representatives of Goldstone and Black Goldstone, add a sense of joy, wonder, and happiness. It is as if thousands of light beams joined together to create a demonstration of illumination. With Hematite's presence, what more could be expected but the spirit's miraculous ability to lighten and brighten the way?

SECTION V
FINAL NOTES UPON COMPLETION

CHAPTER XXVI

CRYSTAL HEALING FOR THE PREVENTION AND TREATMENT OF AIDS

In treating any dis-ease, it is important to look at its root causes. This is especially important when treating AIDS since this dis-ease is essentially affecting everyone on the planet today and is evoking concern on a global level. In light of the fact that this dis-ease has taken on such massive proportion, the lessons that can be learned from it must be enormous as well. In order to understand the root causes of AIDS, we must first examine the psychological-emotional correlations. Even though there is an increasing number of heterosexual men, as well as women and children, that are presently vulnerable to AIDS, we will focus our attention on one of the largest groups of people affected by AIDS to date: gay men. Although the information that follows is far from being complete, I have chosen to present what has been discovered thus far in an effort that this disease might be better understood. In so doing, it is my hope that we can all take one step closer to healing and understanding the lessons that parallel its manifestation.

ROOT CAUSES

As the human race evolves, the forces of polarity will become more unified and complimentary, instead of opposing. The male and female sides of each person will both be expressed, resulting in a more balanced state of human androgyny. If we look at what has happened with the women's movement, as well as the gay movement in the last decade, it is easy to see that this shift is starting to occur. Many men are being born with a more androgynous nature. In the same way, many women are learning to assert themselves in a more balanced manner. It is as if there are genetic codes within our cells that are being triggered now, attracting the circumstances needed in order to create the new way of androgyny.

In this evolutionary process, many men being born with this androgynous nature are suffering the most. According to traditional planetary programming, men have been trained to suppress their feelings and be more warrior like in their approach to life. But what happens when souls that are incarnated into male bodies do not identify with this traditional male programming? The answer is this: the innate nature of those men becomes suppressed when it is condemned by society. They are made to feel that their essential qualities must be wrong.

As a man of this character grows up in the world, he is often forced in early childhood to unwillingly submit and repress his natural instincts. If not, he will be found unacceptable to his family, friends, and society in general. As time passes, his true nature gets stifled and as a result, deep feeling of inadequacy, guilt, shame, and fear develop. In desperately trying to fit into society's limiting definitions, and being unable to do so, the roots of insecurity and inadequacy sink deeper and deeper into his heart. Feeling unworthy in the world of which he is a part creates an inner turmoil that makes him susceptible to manifesting physical dis-ease.

HEALING AND PREVENTION

The healing balm to treat the root cause of AIDS is self-love and self acceptance. The gay male generally has not been taught to love who he is nor to accept his basic nature. It is also necessary for a man with AIDS to make a conscious choice and decide if he is willing to look into the deep inner recesses of his own heart and heal his internal wounds. If so, then there is hope for peace, understanding, and healing. AIDS can be a doorway to ultimate self-empowerment, if he can truly accept who he is, align with his source, and come to understand why he has chosen his path.

The following information can be useful for any person suffering with the AIDS virus, whether or not the individual is gay or heterosexual, man or woman. When working with someone who has AIDS, the most effective Master Crystals to use are Isis Crystals, Time Link Crystals, Window Crystals, and Channeling Crystals. Because clear quartz generally amplifies energy, these crystals should only be used when consciously working with the root causes of the dis-ease. The Isis Crystal will facilitate the powers of self-healing and bring forth the nurturing force of divine femininity. The Time Link Crystal can be used to bridge the aspect of the self who is healed in the future into the present, as well as to connect with the inner child of the past who is in need of the real healing. They can also be used to link into a past life that may be pertinent in understanding why the dis-ease has manifested in this life time. The Window Crystal can be meditated with to reflect the soul's true image and the Channeling Crystal can be used to express the soul's message into spoken words. (See previous chapters and *Crystal Healing*, Vol. II for specific information on these Master Crystals).

One of the hardest predicaments for a person with AIDS is that the chakras are constantly going out of alignment because of the intense fear and pain. The following Chakra Balance Layout is specifically designed for this predicament. It can be practiced for twenty minutes, two or three times a day, either alone or with a facilitator. This layout will be effective in keeping the chakras balanced so that identification with source can be established and the situation can be more consciously dealt with.

The Layout: Place pieces of Hawkeye at the soles of each foot to channel a peaceful healing energy into the body. Place Luvulite on the groin points to strengthen the lymph glands over that area. A piece of Rhodonite is to be placed upon the first chakra point to usher the love from the heart center into the base chakra. Bloodstone, Carnelian, or Red Jasper can be placed at the second chakra to purify the blood. If possible, place a piece of Cuprite on both sides of the second chakra stone to assist with oxygenization. At the navel, place Citrine or Gold Calcite to improve assimilation, strengthen will power, and stimulate the spleen. Place Green Aventurine at the solar plexus to soothe emotional turbulence. At the heart chakra, use as many Rose Quartz stones as desired to encourage self-love. Blue Lace Agate or Amazonite can be placed at the throat chakra to facilitate the expression of true feeling. Amethyst can be used at the third eye to awaken the intuition and assist in soul alignment. Pyrite and Clear or Gold Calcite can be placed at the crown chakra to bring the light into the physical body and encourage mental order.

Follow the therapeutic procedures outlined in *Crystal Healing*, Vol. II and breathe deeply, through the center line, as identification with personal source is established. Once the stones have been placed upon the body, focus upon each successive chakra and breathe in the color of the chakra. Afterward, affirm the alignment that has occurred and visualize complete healing.

If more stones than this are laid upon the body it is important to have a trained crystal healer, familiar with working with AIDS, to facilitate the discovery and release of pent up inner emotions. Any number of things could be released when a full crystal healing layout is performed. It is important that the facilitator be understanding of the situation and be well trained in order to assist in the release and re-programming processes.

THE LESSONS FOR HUMANITY

AIDS is not just a gay dis-ease. It has far ranging effects on all of us. As a race there are several lessons that we all can learn through witnessing AIDS. First, it is teaching everyone on the planet to be more conscious about sexuality. As a whole, we are being forced to become aware of how and why we use our sexual energy. Many people search for love in the sexual act, looking outside of the self for fulfillment. As we find our security in our own inner source, perhaps we could then learn how to be more loving to ourselves and others, to be closer and more intimate, instead of merely seeking sexual gratification.

It is almost as if gay men have become the martyrs for the new androgynous way. Because of their innate sensitivity, these sensitive souls have taken on the burden of changing a patriarchal world. It is time that heterosexual society acknowledges the natural balance of male-female energies within all people and accepts without judgment these natural tendencies, whether a person is straight or gay, black or white, male or female. AIDS is reflecting to the whole human race our ingrained lack of unconditional love and self-destructive tendencies. If we can learn to love and accept people for who they really are, understand how they feel, and allow them to be themselves, birth will be given to the new male, the new female, and the androgynous way.

The bottom line is that when we do not align with our source, and instead try to seek approval and love from outside of ourselves, we are destined to suffer. As we learn to identify with our own Divine Essence and manifest our natural abilities in accordance with that, peace is upon us, whether the physical body ceases to exist, or not. For those suffering with AIDS, there is no easy answer. But there is hope, if the courage is mustered, to go inside and deal with all of the issues. It is like a black hole, but there is light on the other side. Trust that light, whether it leads to healing or the release of the physical body. It will not fail. It will see us through.

CHAPTER XXVII

DEMATERIALIZATION IN ACTION

Strange things have been known to happen when working in the world of crystals. Phenomena often takes place that cannot be explained with our normal rational minds. Yet, it also cannot be denied when the incidents occur within the realm of personal experience. I would like to share with you one of these truly incredible experiences. If you have read or even looked at the cover photo of *Crystal Healing*, Vol. II, you might already be somewhat prepared for this story.

In creating a cover photograph for the second volume, I was working with my publisher, Barbara Somerfield. We were attempting to find an image that would simultaneously represent the earth, the world of crystals, and the healing that can occur when crystals and stones are placed upon the body. Our goal was to have the cover make a visual statement of *Crystal Healing*, (the title of the book). After we had worked unsuccessfully with several different artists and photographers, I approached a local Taos photographer who was referred to me because of her ability to sensitively photograph still objects.

The crystal that we chose to shoot was one that I found several years ago at a gem show and fell in love with, yet chose not to purchase because it was too expensive. The night after I saw the crystal, I dreamt about it and the next morning, I went back to the show and bought it. Much later, I learned that this particular crystal is a Channeling Crystal, a Transmitter Crystal, a Dow, and a Window Crystal. Needless to say, it has become one of my personal teachers. Since then I have worked extensively with it during the process of writing *Crystal Enlightenment*, *Crystal Healing*, and of course it sits here with me now as I write *The Crystalline Transmission*.

Many individual shots were taken of this crystal, with the sky and the earth as backgrounds. Composites were made of some of them and they were taken to Barbara in New York City for final review. Seeing the slides of all the shots taken, there was no question which one would be the best suited to meet our goals. The one and only slide of this particular shot was then wisked off to the cover artist to prepare it for printing.

Now, I must admit that I was very late getting the second volume completed, mostly because I needed to thoroughly understand the information myself before putting it out into the world. Whatever the reasons, the manuscript was several months late, despite all the prior commitments that had been made assuring distributors and bookstores that it would be out in October of 1987. As it turned out, its own perfect birth-time was January of 1988. Nevertheless, business time does not always relate to 'perfect time' and there was intense pressure in businessville to have the material available to the public sooner, rather than later.

A few days later Barbara called in a state of dismay and said, "The slide is missing!" I said, "What do you mean, the slide is missing?" To which she responded, "The cover artist had it, was working with it and it just disappeared. She has had her office combed by several people, has looked everywhere, and it just cannot be found. What do you think is going on?"

Since both Barbara and I had several experiences that gave us the distinct impression that there were forces that definitely did not want this work to get out, my first thought was 'the dark forces must have taken it!' But, since one of the topics in the soon to be released book was 'Demate-rialization' (see *Crystal Healing*, Vol. II, page 170), I decided to tune into the situation a little more. Holding the teacher crystal (that had been photographed) in one hand and my most powerful Window Crystal in the other, I placed the perfect diamond shaped window to the teacher crystal and felt a strong current of energy being transmitted. I then put the Window Crystal to my third eye and received this message:

"NO, the dark forces, as you define them, are not in-volved. The slide has literally dematerialized, has gone into a pure crystalline state and will return. When it does, the lighting will be significantly different on it, DO NOT CHANGE IT, for it will embody a Crystal Deva which will serve a great purpose in the fulfillment of this work. It will return in time. "

I said, "In time?! What does that mean? Your time? My time? By Christmas time? The printers time???" But there was no further response, that was the end of the transmission.

I called my publisher back and gave her the message. Since it was all that we had to go on, we both accepted it. By this time the cover artist had been hypnotized and would get to the point in her session where the slide was right there with her, and then it was just gone. Understanding that this woman was not metaphysically oriented, and feeling compassion for her frustration and anxiety over the matter, I sat with my teacher crystal once again and asked for guidance. This is what I received:

"Since a Crystal Deva is being born onto the earth plane through the medium of this photograph, why not assist in her birth? "

Acting as midwives, myself in New Mexico and my publisher in New York, we simultaneously set up crystal altars and dedicated time to the rebirth of the slide. I put my teacher crystal in the center of my altar and surrounded it with Black Tourmaline to help the Deva get grounded, Selenite to usher in its light body, Rose Quartz to lend a loving hand, Amethyst to create mental peace, and Gem Silica to provide nurturing feminine energy. I spent the rest of the day focussed on the rematerialization of the slide and the birth of the Crystal Deva.

I would not have been surprised if the slide reappeared on my altar. But instead, several hours later I got a call from Barbara who excitedly reported that the slide had been recovered in the cover artist's office, in a place previously searched. I asked if there were any visible changes on it and she told me that it was filthy and that they wouldn't really be able to tell until it was cleaned and converted into the actual cover photograph. The first covers were printed December 23, 1987.

The telephone calls that followed in the next week were truly amazing. I would hear daily of the transformations that were occurring in the photograph. Being metaphysically oriented, and trusting the information that had been given to us, we expected to find some vague representation of a Crystal Deva. Neither one of us were prepared to find dozens of beings materializing in the golden center line that had appeared in the slide. The golden center line itself was a phenomenon since one of the therapeutic techniques discussed in *Crystal Healing*, Vol. II is the 'Center Line Focus' which is used to help the receiver of a crystal healing focus on his/her own golden lighted center. Forming out of that radiant center in the photograph was a yogi sitting upon a lotus, a space being, an Egyptian pharaoh and numerous other entities. When the photograph was turned upside down, a Chinese Sage, a representation of the Divine Mother, an owl, and many other beings were witnessed.

All right, what was going on here?! In an attempt to find out before the book hit the streets, Barbara flew to New Mexico the day before I was to leave for Egypt to do personal research on Volume III. When she arrived, with dozens of copies of the phenomenal cover photo in hand, we sat down and surrounded ourselves with them. We placed the teacher crystal in front of us, along with many other Channeling Crystals, Transmitter Crystals, and large generators. We then opened ourselves to find out what was going on. This is what we received:

"This photograph is serving as an interdimensional gateway for many representations of that you would define as 'masters. ' Whether or not one reads the material contained within the book, if one merely glances at the cover, these beings are available, if the individual so chooses, to assist in the healing process. For those who will study and use the material for personal or professional purposes, these beings will serve to protect and guide. There are also obvious lessons offered through the medium of this photograph in the art of interdimensional travel and dematerialization. "

I guess there was!! The week that the slide disappeared and reappeared I had several personal experiences with things literally dematerializing on me. For example, I had written an article for a magazine and had submitted it a week before, complete with pictures. Around the same time that the slide disappeared I received a call from the magazine's editor informing me that the article and the pictures were missing.

"What do you mean missing?" I asked in a state of disbelief.

"Just gone, we have no idea where they disappeared to. Can you send us another copy?"

I did and all was well. Later that week, I was doing errands around town. My last stop was the bank where I went to the drive up window, got my deposit out of my purse, and made the transaction without getting out of my car. When I returned home, my purse was missing. Mentally retracing my steps, I realized that it too had probably dematerialized. I started to take this whole thing very personally and must admit that I let the universe know that I was not very happy. In need of the personal belongings in my purse, I called the bank. The teller told me that my purse had been found safe and sound inside of the bank. I then demanded to know what was going on from the universe.

It took a couple of weeks and a trip to Egypt to gain perspective on the matter. Now I see it as one of my main lessons and challenges, one that the crystals are here to demonstrate and teach. The crystals, being pure expressions of spirit and matter, simultaneously exist in the realms of light while manifesting on a physical level. They can easily zip back and forth, from matter into spirit and from the earth plane into the realms of light. I have witnessed the fact that it is possible and that it does happen.

My week of experiencing the realities of dematerialization in action was only a small lesson which we are all learning. ANYTHING IS POSSIBLE!! We have become so limited by our beliefs that the physical world is governed by a certain set of linear laws. Our programmed thinking confirms this reality. I was taught during that incredible week that IT IS POSSIBLE for things to zip from one dimension to another. If it is possible for crystals, (and other inanimate objects) why wouldn't it be possible for us as humans, with the aid of our own wills, to consciously go anywhere we put our minds to? Why not think, believe and know ourselves to be in a world that is founded upon peace and joy? Why limit ourselves to what we have heard and been programmed to believe as true? Instead, let's open up our minds and create the thoughts that we can truly be healed, aligned, attuned, and at one with the Divine Essence. That reality is also present at every moment for us to draw upon, to literally create what we have traditionally learned to define as miracles.

In sharing this phenomenal story with you, I also lead you to observe for yourself the cover photograph of Volume II. Meditate on it when you start to doubt and let it serve as physical plane proof that there are masters and entities that are working with you, that they are aspects of yourself. Know that these beings are guiding and protecting the emergence of crystal healing onto this planet. This photo is alive with presence. It has representatives from all major spiritual paths. Being that a very eclectic group is using this photograph as a landing pad, there is someone residing therein that everyone can relate to.

When the book was tested in England with a very sophisticated machine that registers energy fields, it showed that this multidimensional photograph has an auric field as strong as a human's. The answers and the explanations lay beyond the realms of our programmed reality. Yet, there it is, undeniably present on the physical plane for all to see. It is a statement unto itself that there is much more going on than what can be explained with a limited belief system. The photograph at this point for me is a strong symbol of hope, that we can, and will, embrace our potential to live our highest destiny as human light-beings.

CHAPTER XXVIII

NUCLEAR RADIATION ASSIMILATION

The energies on our earth are rapidly accelerating. It is becoming increasingly important for each of us to learn how to assimilate and integrate those frequencies. Many cycles are being completed within the next decade. The earth is undergoing tremendous shifts as it strives to come into total alignment with the great central sun. In much the same way, we as conscious life forms upon the earth's surface, are striving to align our beings with the Divine Essence at our Stellar Gateway Chakra. As we prepare to close not only a century, but a 2,000 year age, as well as a 26,000 year cycle, we are being exposed to a massive amount of higher frequency energy. This energy can be used to thrust us into new beginnings if we can learn to assimilate it into our beings.

Nuclear radiation emits a vast array of energy frequencies, most of which cannot be assimilated by the human system. The human race is constantly being exposed to these energies due to nuclear accidents and unprotected nuclear wastes. Even though our eyes are not capable of seeing the entire electromagnetic spectrum of rays that nuclear radiation emits, they nevertheless exist. Some of these shorter-than-light wavelengths (ultra-violet) and longer-than-light wavelengths (infra-red) easily pass through physical plane matter. When they pass through human bodies, they often throw the system out of alignment and the organic structure begins to break down. Thus, all life suffers from the devastating effects of nuclear radiation.

But, what would happen if our physical bodies were able to assimilate these higher frequency energies? What if our light bodies resided within our physical bodies and elevated the vibration of matter? Would the effects of nuclear radiation then have a positive, instead of a negative effect? I suspect so. This has been a theory of mine since I conceived the idea of the Crystalline Transmission. Of course only time and circumstances will tell. In the meantime, play with the idea. It is possible.

NATURALLY RADIATED CRYSTALS TO THE RESCUE!

There are several crystals that have been exposed to electromagnetic radiation in their natural growth process and have not only survived, but have become more valuable because of it. The most important ones for our purposes are Smoky Quartz, Kunzite, Aquamarine, and Emerald. These crystals can be used in crystal healing layouts, worn, carried, meditated with, or taken in gem remedies. They will strengthen the auric field and stabilize the physical system in order to provide protection against the present damaging effects of nuclear radiation.

The dark color found in Smoky Quartz is caused by natural radiation within the earth. Man-made smoky quartz on the other hand, is made by exposing clear quartz to x-rays. This synthetic version cannot be used for the same purpose as the naturally radiated Smoky Quartz because of the artificial means through which it is created. In its authentic state, Smoky Quartz will help to ground the essence of the light body into the first chakra. Containing the highest amount of light force in a dark color, Smoky Quartz will serve to lay the foundation upon which higher frequency energies can safely manifest in the physical body. Smoky Quartz will also assist in dissolving negative thoughts and emotions that can make the physical body even more susceptible to negative outside influences.

Kunzite serves a most important purpose in the assimilation of higher frequency energy as it fortifies the heart chakra with incredible strength. With the heart open and activated, a strong force field will result which will serve as a natural protective shield. Being a soft purple-pink ray, Kunzite has a special calming effect upon both the thoughts and the emotions. Mental-emotional equilibrium will further create an aura that cannot easily be bombarded by external energies. Being striated, Kunzite will strengthen the physical body, as well as the heart chakra to allow for the assimilation of an influx of higher energy.

Aquamarine is for expression of the highest truth at the throat chakra. As the light body descends into the physical body, it is necessary that its radiance be brought into full expression. Aquamarine will serve to open up the avenues for verbal manifestation of spirit. Since blue is the peace ray, Aquamarine will calm and cool the effects of radiation with its soft tranquil color.

Emerald is the best stone to use to relieve suffering due to exposure of excess radiation. Its deep verdant color penetrates into all levels of the body, heart, and mind. As it does, the green ray helps to heal and rejuvenate damaged cells and tissues. Emerald is also a strong companion to take along when traveling through areas that are known to have nuclear plants or toxic waste products. Worn over the heart chakra, Emerald will strengthen the thymus gland which in turn will fortify the immune system for increased protection and healing.

The human race is in the process of adjusting to many forces. It is mandatory that we learn how to adapt to the higher energy fields that we are constantly being exposed to. If we can, it is possible to evolve, to mutate if you will, in order to meet the growing needs of a new tomorrow. If we can apply the Crystalline Transmission to our lives, we will be assured of hope for the future. When we learn to integrate and assimilate the force of light, a new spectrum will open up to us, one that encompasses infra-red and ultra-violet.

CHAPTER XXIX

EARTHKEEPER ACTIVATION

Since the original information about The Earthkeepers was written in *Crystal Healing*, Vol. II, amazing advancements have been made in the process of activating one of these awesome crystal giants. To briefly review, The Earthkeepers are enormous quartz crystals, averaging three and a half to seven feet in length and weighing up to 8,500 pounds. These crystals were created many thousands of years ago by the non-physical Elders of our race when they beamed their light force into the silicon dioxide of the earth. The Earthkeepers served to magnetize the force field of the earth in preparation for the birth of conscious life forms upon this planet. As human evolution began its natural descent into the illusionary world of the senses, the Earthkeeper Crystals were buried deep within the ground and were programmed to record the entire cycle of human evolution. They have now resurfaced and require specialized attunement and attention in order to be activated. Once activated, the Earthkeepers will serve two important functions. First, they will transmit the cumulative knowledge of the entire earth plane cycle back to the stellar realms to be used for the development of consciousness on other worlds. Secondly, the Earthkeepers will transmit the consciousness of the Elders upon the earth, enabling all those who come into their presence to be uplifted and inspired. (Please read pages 155-164 in Volume II for complete information on the Earthkeepers).

EARTHKEEPER

EARTHKEEPER

THE CRYSTALLINE
TRANSMISSION
A Synthesis of Light

Crystal Academy
P.O. Box 1334
Kapaa, Hawaii 96746

http://webcrystalacademy.com

808 823-6959 FX 808 821-1165

KATRINA RAPHAELL

CHAPTER XXX

COMPLETION

It has been a most remarkable experience writing the Crystal Trilogy, one that I am indeed grateful for. From the beginning, this work has been guided and directed by forces that I have learned to trust implicitly. It was relayed to me, before *Crystal Enlightenment* was written, that this trilogy would manifest and that through it, ancient knowledge would be brought to the masses. Many years later, I now know that the knowledge contained within all three books is not mine, even though I served as a vehicle for the writing. It belongs to everyone that identifies with it. Now that the trilogy has been completed I see more clearly how each volume has served its particular purpose.

Crystal Enlightenment, Volume I gave not only the information concerning many crystals and stones, it served to relay certain concepts that each stone demonstrates. For example, when we think of Rose Quartz we automatically relate to self-love. When we look at Gem Silica, our minds identify with feminine nurturing energy and expanded perspectives. When we hold Azurite to the third eye we cannot help but be encouraged to clear the cobwebs of fear from our subconscious minds. In this way the crystals and stones have shared vital new concepts that we are using in our personal process of healing and reprogramming.

Crystal Healing, Volume II is about healing ourselves by using the Ancient Art of Laying On Of Stones. Specific therapeutics are taught that enable a crystal healing to serve its ultimate purpose. By assisting each person who receives a healing to first align with Divine Essence, insight is attained and healing occurs. Volume II also discusses six Master Crystals which can be used in various ways to accelerate our evolutionary process.

Finally, *The Crystalline Transmission*, Volume III takes us full circle as we realize that the crystals and stones have served to teach us how to align with our own inner crystalline light force. With the means given to activate the twelve chakra system, the Crystalline Transmission becomes a living reality as we literally integrate the light body into the physical body. The Predominant Power Stones as well as the final six Master Crystals provide us with additional tools with which we can further empower ourselves.

With the completion of the Crystal Trilogy, I too, am completing a major life cycle. It is time for me to not be so intimately identified with crystals. Oh yes, they will always be around me and a vital part of my life. But, it is now time for me to walk, breathe, and live the Crystalline Transmission to the best of my ability. What comes after this? I am not sure. But I do know that it will be in divine order and that there is more to come.

ACKNOWLEDGEMENTS

I would like to acknowledge and thank the following people for their assistance and support in writing this book.

Sananda Ra	Support, Encouragement, Inspiration, Assistance With Cathedral Lightbraries
Simran Raphaell	For Sharing His Mother With The World
Andrea Cagan	Support, Encouragement, Understanding, Assistance Accessing Information For The Time Link Crystals
Stephanie Nemett	Editing, Personal Support, Assistance in Compiling AIDS Information

The Crystalline Transmission

Gurudeva and Siva Ceyon Swami	Assistance in Gathering Information on Devic Temple Crystals and Earthkeeper Activation
Eric Starwalker	Assistance in Gathering Information on The Tantric Twin Crystals
Jane Ann Dow	Assistance in Gathering Information on The Dow Crystals
Martha Smith	Personal Support and Encouragement
Pam and Winnie Parker Larry Audette	Assistance in Gathering Miscellaneous Information
Sandra Orgel	For Her Special Sensitivity in Illustrating The Diagrams
Nora Stewart	Photographs of Crystals
Gail Russell	Photograph of Katrina
Isabel Lugo	Personal Support and Assistance
The Mattsson Family	Unconditional Love and Support
Drunvalo Melchizedek	Consultation and Information

ABOUT THE AUTHOR

Katrina Raphaell has worked in the New Age Healing Arts for over sixteen years. After extensive training and practice, she then taught varied aspects of the healing arts such as massage, iridology, kineseology, homeopathy, herbology, flower essences, and nutrition. With a background in nursing, she also served as the Director of Health Care for a natural drug and alcohol rehabilitation program. Throughout her studies and healing practices, Katrina became very aware of the mental and emotional imbalances that were always related to physical dis-ease. As the world of crystals opened up to her, she became more aware of the powers of light and color in working on the subtle aspects of the being. Through years of experience in various forms of yoga and meditation, Katrina attuned her mind to the vibrational language of the mineral kingdom and perceived the crystal's wisdom. Applying first hand information based on what she received in her personal meditations, experience and expertise were gained which led to the information now available in her books.

Katrina is known as the leading authority in the crystal field. Her books, *Crystal Enlightenment Vol. I, Crystal Healing, Vol. II,* and *The Crystalline Transmission, Vol. III,* are published in many countries around the world. In order to facilitate the art of crystal healing, Katrina opened the Crystal Academy of Advanced Healing Arts, in Taos, New Mexico in 1986 where she has certified hundreds of people from around the world. Katrina's Crystal Trilogy has brought to light ancient healing practices and methods for achieving greater wholeness and expanded consciousness.

For further information and a brochure of current certification courses please write:

KATRINA RAPHAELL
The Crystal Academy
PO Box 1334
Kapaa Kuai, Hawaii 96746
Tel. 808 823-6959 Fax 808 821-1165

KATRINA RAPHAELL

CRYSTAL ENLIGHTENMENT

The Transforming Properties of Crystals and Healing Stones

Katrina Raphaell

KATRINA RAPHAELL

This book is a comprehensive, yet easy to understand guide to the use of crystals and gems for internal growth, healing and balance in your daily life. Discover new resources, learn how to extend your personal awareness and center by attuning to crystal energies. The magnitude and potential of crystals and gems to impact positively our personal lives and the evolving planet we live on is significant.

Some of the topics explored in this book are:

- What are crystals physically and esoterically?
- Working with crystals for self-healing
- The ancient art of laying on stones
- Psychic Protection
- Generator Crystals
- Important healing stones and their uses
- Double terminated stones and their functions
- Crystal Meditations
- Black Holes

Crystal Enlightenment is designed for the lay person, as well as the professional, to give the basic understanding necessary to use the healing properties inherent within the mineral kingdom to improve the quality of our external and internal lives.

ISBN: 0-943358-27-2   Paperback   5½×8½   175 Pages

CRYSTAL HEALING

The Therapeutic Application Of Crystals and Stones
Katrina Raphaell

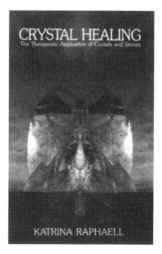

Volume Two of the Crystal Trilogy further refines the practical applications of crystal therapeutic techniques. Katrina introduces innovative, previously unavailable methods for discovering and removing internal imbalances. This wealth of information derived from the author's first-hand experience is practical, while inviting the reader to explore deeper levels and gain insight into the processes underlying our disease and health patterns.

Unique in its content, **Crystal Healing** reveals for the first time:

- 6 Master Crystals
- Time Bridging
- Maintenance-Personal Responsibility
- Exorcising
- Past/Future Life Recall
- Laser Wands
- Protection & Guidance
- Conscious Reprogramming
- Mind, Body, Heart & Soul Correlations
- Window Crystals
- Dematerialization
- Channeling Crystals

To facilitate a complete understanding of the specific techniques described, **Crystal Healing** is strikingly illustrated with detailed color photographs. Step-by-step instructions encourage an understanding of all you need to know to reap the benefits emanating through crystals and stones. This invaluable guide enables the lay person and professional to use crystals and healing stones for soul activation, complete healing and expansion of consciousness. In addition to the information in **Volume One**, this book will help activate hidden potential and open up a world of light into your life.

ISBN: 0-943358-30-2 **Paperback** 5½×8½ **220 Pages**

AURORA PRESS

Aurora Press is devoted to pioneering books that catalyze personal growth, balance and transformation. It aims to make available, in a digestible format, an innovative synthesis of ancient wisdom and twentieth century resources, integrating esoteric knowledge and daily life. Aurora titles specialize in astrology, health, metaphysical philosophies, and the emerging global consciousness.

For our online catalog
& ordering info, visit,
www.AuroraPress.com

Aurora Press
PO Box 573
Santa Fe, N.M. 87504

Fax 505 982-8321
www.AuroraPress.com
Email: Aurorep@aol.com

Credit Card Orders Only
Fax 734 995-8535
Tel. 888 894-8621